Elf Quotes

A Collection of Over 1000 Ancient Elven Sayings and Wise Elfin Koans by The Silver Elves About Magic and The Elven Way

The Silver Elves

ISBN-13: 978-1539828778

ISBN-10: 1539828778
Printed in the United States of America by CreateSpace

DEDICATION

This book is dedicated to all our starry sisters and brothers and to the Elven Way.

"This book is an act of magic. It is not really paper
but Starlight you are holding in your hands."
—The Silver Elves. . . . .

"If you think that we are just dreamers,
you must be a figment of our imagination."
—Old Elven Saying

Table of Contents

Introduction

Contained in this book are our original elfin koans, ancient sayings, and other quotes on the Elven Way. Our readers may recognize in *Elf Quotes* many of their favorite "old elven sayings" from our Silver Elves books because we have included with it all of our side-quotes that we have published throughout the years in our Silver Elves books (37 books to this date) on elven magic and enchantment.

Originally, we got the idea to create this book when a fairie sister told us that she wished she had one single book that was a collection of all our side quotes of old elven sayings and ancient wisdom koans from our Silver Elves books so that she could take it with her for inspiration on a very difficult personal journey that she was making. So in this book, we have compiled almost all our sidequotes from our books and have even added many new quotes that have not yet been published in our books. We hope you enjoy reading all of them and sharing them with others. And if perhaps you take this book with you on a personal journey of your own, we wish you blessings and may your way be always illuminated by the Shining Ones.

Kyela,

The Silver Elves

"WHY DOES THE BLIND MAN WALK IN THE DARK
HOLDING HIS LANTERN HIGH?".....
—**Ancient Elven Riddle**

The Elves Say:
"If You Do Not Have the Courage To Be Yourself,
Who Will You Be?"

Ancient Elven Sayings

℘

"FATE IS OUR GUIDE, DESTINY OUR DIRECTION". . . . .

If the waters of the great mountain were only to trickle down, there would be no great ocean.

We elven call our stories Faerie tales, where as most people call their fantasies, history.

One of the primary rules of Elven Society is 'obey yours'elf.'

We are told that the truth cannot be found in books but we Elfin disagree, it is the bookmark.

The elves say the best way to 'save the day' is to party till dawn.

You can not be in touch with your own nature without being in touch with greater nature.

We'd never lie to you. Except for your own good.

The only way to see one's faults is to look at them.

Ultimately life is not a struggle between us and them but us and ours'elves.

Illusions are strongest when spun with the truth.

We can't change our past but we can shape our future.

Those who are eager to change everything at once are usually too impatient to put in the effort to make it last forever.

"The truth belongs to everyone."
—Old Elven Saying

"ONE ELF IS A TORCH. TWO A BEACON LIGHT. THREE DO MAKE A CIRCLE AND FOUR THE DANCE BEGINS.". . . . .

Sometimes if you ask the elves what they are doing they will say everything.

If I knew then what I know now, I wouldn't be so ignorant at this moment.

"Perfection can only be obtained by a never ending effort to achieve it."
—Old Elven Saying

You do not have to be on top of the mountain to know there is something beyond it.

If the truth was easy to recognize there are some folk who'd still go about in disguise.

The Elven say: "It's not who you know that counts so much as how well you know them."

The wind from a Dragon's flight stirs everything.

"An empty head nearly always seeks to fill itself through its mouth."
—Old Elfin Saying.

Every bird has its own song.

The new is often just the old in disguise.

"Neglect neither the great nor the small. And in all things do your best and the best will always come from that." —Old Elven Saying

If you are looking for the elves, They will find you.

The subtle masks the profound.
—Old Elven Saying

Old Elven Saying: They say that if you eat the food of Faerie that you will be trapped there. The fact is, our food is made of Love and once someone eats it, they don't want to leave.

"FAITH IS BORN OF A MARRIAGE OF HOPE AND EXPERIENCE.". . . . .

Proper technique can move mountains that power can not budge.

"Power is best used in the hands of the Fair." Ancient Elven Saying

A bridge is two worlds embracing.

The goal of the path is to travel.

Perfection is an eternal journey, not a finite destination.

Mere words do not wash one's actions clear.

Elves say, "When the Great Mystery begins to make sense, you're probably misunderstanding it."

Healing begins with a wish.

"When you trim off all the fat, the muscle starts to worry." —What the Elves say.

"A leaf doesn't hang up; it hangs out and down." —Old Elven Saying

Whatever you do to the least of us, you do to us all.

All things are illusion save the One thing that is Naught.

"Life is as magical as you make it." —Old Elven Saying

Beware of people who are always sure of themselves. They're probably crazy.

Elvin Saying: Fate is the spouse of Destiny. Like most married folk, they sometimes have their difficulties.

The Elven say: "It is far more important to eat well than eat often."

Failure cannot find those who never give up.

"The elves say the greatest cosmetic is happiness."
—Words of Wisdom by the Eldars

Wisdom of the Eldar

"AN ELF'S PROMISE IS MORE SOLID AND DEPENDABLE THAN THE ROCK OF THE AGES." . . . . .

The Eldar say: "It is just when you think you have mastered a situation that the true test comes."

Some people think elves were a people that once were but are no more. Others think that we never existed. But the truth is the long history and legend of the elves has just begun.

There are many who accuse us fae of being malicious, capricious, and cruel but it is not we who have so callously killed the living forests for profit.

It can be risky at times to dance in the world and a smile is often suspect. But if we don't take a chance with a skip and a prance, our own hearts will always regret.

How can we be but humble when faced with the vast beauty and immensity of the Creation of the Divine Nature. How can we be but thankful for being allowed to share in that Creation in however so small a way.

It is a wise sailor that accepts the fickleness of the wind.

Ritual is the art of repeating one'self with style.

Empires seek to divide and conquer; We elves seek to unite and party.

An elf can be a king or queen among the Elfin. All it takes is absolute devotion to our people. —Wisdom of the Eldar

We honor our ancestors best not by following their ways exactly but by doing what they did better.

When people tell the elves that they feel like someone has walked over their grave, the Eldar say: "It is their own true s'elves calling them from Faerie."

"THE ELVES SAY THE TREE OF LIFE IS A FOREST." —ANCIENT ELVEN KNOWLEDGE OF THE ELDAR. . . . .

The Eldar say: "The loss of one's body is a small thing, the loss of one's soul is everything."

The Eldar say: "The inner teachers can only be studied by experience."

Bureaucracies are the refuge of the incompetent.

The greatest sages are wise enough not to be all knowing.

The truth can be painful, but is far less expensive than deceiving ourselves.

Elves say that truth is both absolute and relative. It is absolutely relative and relatively absolute.

We elves have ancient souls and spirits that are ever young.

A fool that ignores the words of the wise will surely be taught by Life's lash.

It is the nature of the foolish to think themselves wise. It is the privilege of the Wise to watch in silence while life teaches the fool things that mere words never could.

"The path to wisdom is littered with foolish choices." Olde Elven Saying.

There is a difference between ignorance and folly. All of us are ignorant of some things but a fool clings to his ignorance as though it were his last penny.

When the elves speak of the Edar, we are often referring to our ancestors; although since we practice reincarnation, we are sometimes referring to modern elves as well.

Elves are as old as the stars and young as the new dawn.

What Say the Elves About The Elven Way

"THE ELVEN WAY PASSES BEYOND THE FIELDS OF THE KNOWN INTO THE UNKNOWN ILLUMINATED BY THE GLOW OF THE ELVES." . . . . .

We call it the Elven Way but we could call it the Faerie Way, the Fair Way, the Way of the Fae, the Way of the Shining Ones, or even the Way that begins in your Dreams and ends in the Life Magical.

The Elven Way is not only the Way of the elves but the Way to Elfin.
—Ancient Elfin Knowledge

In the long run it does not matter how you get there as long as you do get there, and yet if you don't choose the right Way for you, you will get lost again and again. This is a paradox of the Elven Way but one with which elves become increasingly comfortable and in doing so find the Way ever more easily.

The Way is individual but always considers what is fair for everyone.

One might ask if the elves are such unique individuals how can they travel the Way together. And the answer is, "Quite Easily!"

When we say the Elven Way, we do not mean one path that each and all must tread without exception save that each finds hir own creative expression in harmony with life and creates thus hir own true Elven Way.

What does it take to tread the Elven Way? Everything you have. All of your heart, all of your soul, and all that you do every night and day.

The Way to Elfin is found on the path to one's on true s'elf.

Unlike many others, Elves do not hire mercenaries to fight our battles for us. Those of us who believe in a cause Fight for it. That is our way.

The elves say the Path is like a tree growing in all directions at the same time.

"WE ELVES AND FAERIES ARE OFTEN PORTRAYED AS DANCING IN A CIRCLE. THIS IS BOTH BECAUSE WE SEE LIFE AS A DANCE AND BECAUSE THE ELVEN WAY GOES EVER ON." . . . . .

We elves are not shocked when someone abandons the Elven Way. Individuals have been wandering in and out of faerie nearly forever. Yet we ever await their return, or we are confident that once someone has experienced love and magic, they will eventually want more of it. This is not to say that elfin magic is addictive, just amazingly irresistible.

The problem with trying to explain to people about our elven ways is that we don't really have any beyond living with love and compassion and style.

The way of the elves is quite simple. They say be yourself, do your magic in harmony with Nature and the Divine and encourage others to do the same. And all things shall in time turn out perfectly and as they were always meant to, which is to say, as we've ever desired and wished them to be.

While most people divide the world between what is beautiful and what is ugly, elves see the beauty in nearly everything and yet ever seek to make all things more lovely.

If you desire to describe the elves, you cannot go for wrong in using the words enchanting and original.

The elfin strive to find enjoyment, pleasure and humor in nearly every circumstance, even if, at times, it is only the anomaly of the situation that amuses us.

The Elven Way is not a religion or a cult. It could be described as a movement but it is probably best understood as a dance.

We elfin follow the way of Nature. Ours is the path of least resistance, which is the law of Nature. Some might take that to mean that we are submissive or easily dominated, but in truth, it indicates that we assist all beings in their quest toward fulfillment, including the wicked whom we aid in their head long rush toward destruction, by redirecting their energy away from the innocent and toward their own selves.

Elven society is not competitive. Every individual is encouraged and empowered to be successful.

The Elven Speak About the Trees, Earth, and Nature

"A TREE WITHOUT ROOTS CANNOT LIVE; A TREE WITHOUT BRANCHES DOES NOT CARE TO." . . . . .

The Sylvan Elves consider the trees to be their elder brothers and sisters who shelter, feed and protect them.

Elven cities are so filled with trees, vines, bushes, and flowers that they are nearly always indistinguishable from a forest.

The Elvish say: "If the Earth did not love us, she would not feed us."

We've heard men say they will hunt someone down to the ends of the Earth. Apparently they are unaware that it is round.

Some folks think we elves worship trees. That is not quite accurate, but we do adore them.

We elves are often associated with the trees, the stars, the sea, the moonlight, mountain fastnesses and crystal caves. This is not only because these are places we come from but because they are sources of great magic.

We elves don't make magic so much as channel it from wondrous Nature that lives all around.

"Each tree finds its path to the light." —Ancient Elfin Wisdom

It is not simply that the trees are alive that we mourn their passing but that they are so beautiful. And when we consider that men destroy them to build ugly boxes to live within which while giving shade, cool them not at all, we are deeply puzzled

Elves relate to most trees far better than we get along with most normal folk.

"ELVES CONSIDER NATURE AS THE GREATEST SCIENTIST FOR IT IS EVER EXPERIMENTING." —ANCIENT ELVEN KNOWLEDGE. . . . .

We elves consider the winds talented musicians. They can play chimes. They can play the aeolean harp. But perhaps their greatest instrument is the leaves on the trees.

Wherever we elven move, we first introduce ours'elves to the local flora, fauna and various elementals. That way, before we've ever met a single person, we've already made friends in the area.

Every tree in Elfland is born of a dream and bears the fruit and seeds of many more.

The woodland elves say that every leaf tells a story and every tree reveals the secrets of the Universe.

"The Forest is the Trees." —Elven Saying

The spirits speak to us in living nature. We just need to watch and listen.

If the wind howls, howl with it.

"Every tree is a unique expression of its kind." Olde Elven Saying meaning: You don't have to be totally different from everyone, you just have to be true to your own nature.

It is said that the trees learned to speak from the elves and when they did they taught us wondrous things.

Unlike some folks, we elfin do not view ours'elves as being separate from nature but rather as part of it. We are not striving to rise above nature but to harmonize with it. We know that there are elements of nature that would prey upon us but we do not interpret that to mean that all of nature is against us. But rather that we have still a ways to go in our mastery of magic. As far as we're concerned, we have everything we need to create Faerie on Earth... which we do in our lives everyday.

We could be a leaf all day long but we'll eventually fall from the tree, but if we are the tree itself, we'll live eternally through the flowering of the seeds.

"TO THE ELVES ALL BEINGS ARE PERSONS. HORSES, TREES, PLANTS, BIRDS, EVEN THE EARTH ITSELF IS GREETED POLITELY.".....

In Elfin, even the trees do magic.

There is not much that disturbs the elves but the unwarranted destruction of the trees infuriates us.

If you ask the elves what celebrities they admire most, they will likely say: "The Trees."

Sometimes we hear of people trying to save this or that faery tree from road builders but the truth is if it were up to the elves we wouldn't let them cut down a single tree unless it was already dead.

Among the Elven, even the tree stumps are revered.

Tolkien wrote that the elves were the fairest and wisest of all beings but the elves say that of the trees.

Some people think it never rains in Elfin but, of course, it does. Where else would we get rainbows and the mists of Faerie? Although, it is true, the rains in Elfin are healing and magical.

"Nature adorns us." Olde Elven Saying.

Elves truly love man and his Kind but not as much as we love the Trees.

Trees in the Forest don't grow in rows. Thus the Path is seldom straight.

All of Nature conspires to move us toward becoming our own true s'elves.

"Every plant blossoms when the conditions are favorable." —Olde Elven Saying

Elves Speak About Death, Necromancy, Reincarnation, Immortality and Eternity

"WHEN WE ELVES HEAR SOMEONE SAY THEY WISH THEY WERE YOUNG AGAIN, WE THINK, 'JUST WAIT'!". . . . .

We have one life and many bodies.

"Eternity is always approached through the Present." Elfish Saying

Men say you only have one life to live. Elves say you only have one life to live at a time.

Immortality is a function not of the body but of the consciousness.

In the end, we die as we were born and as we elves have ever lived, embracing the Mystery.

The beginning holds all that comes after. The End contains all that came before. Time is Eternal and it is always Now.

To the elves, the future and the past are one. They each contain something wondrous to embrace.

"Immortality is a function not of the body but of the consciousness."
—Elven Wisdom.

We elven are a devoted folk; we are devoted to love, laughter and having a good time. From these stem healing, magic and ultimately immortality.

The path of the Elfin never ends for it is the Way to Immortality.

Some people think Life and Death are opposites, Elves know they are the same.

The Elfin say: "While our bodies may grow old, our spirits remain eternal."

*"WE HAVE COME TO TAKE OUR BODIES TO GIVE OUR SPIRITS BIRTH." —
ELVEN SONG LYRIC. . . . .*

When someone passes from their body, the elves guide them through the Great Forest to anew life in Faerie.

Elves can live a very long time and in good health, but when a body does begin to fail, we never say we are dying; we say instead, "I'm shedding."

The only time is now, which is eternally transforming. The place is here, which is everywhere.

We elves are immortal, not because we live forever, but because we share in the Life Divine.

We appear to be much younger than we really are and normal folk who are younger than us appear so very much older. But then that is the key to our "immortality". It is by staying young that we grow old.

Mayhaps the essence of the difference between the philosophies of the elves and that of men is this: Men think there is nothing more permanent than Death. While we elves think there is nothing more transitory.

What is the point of Necromancy if not to see the way things were in the past so we will know what's likely to be in the now.

The Elven Say:
"Every time we come near death we hear our ancestors say, hang on, cling to life, cherish every moment. This perhaps is the most common necromancy there is and nearly everyone experiences it."

Realities of Elfin: "Even death cannot make us forget our elven lovers."

The waters of the Eternal Spring of Elfin don't make one immortal; they enable one to see that one *is* immortal.

Death is just the sleep of a lifetime.

"Death is not the opposite of Life, it is the means Life uses to change." . . . . .

Elves believe in re-incarnation, thus they say in honoring our ancestors,
we honor ourselves.

"The Voices of the ancestors rise from the land, waft through the trees, sing from the water, the incessant song of Necromancy." —Elven Knowledge

Life begins through replication and continues through diversity. The Source is the same but the experience different and the possibilities nearly infinite. The deepest necromancy doesn't call to the dead but to the source that connects us all.

"Some folks think they are speaking to the Dead. We elves know there are no dead, there are only those who have transformed." —Ancient Elven Wisdom

Men say that history repeats itself, but really it is we who out of habit and obstinacy repeat the same mistakes over and over again. One of the great values of Necromancy is to see how things were in the past and change them.

"We are necromancers. We summon the dead, to inform the living and shape those yet to be who were and are and always will be."
— The Necromancers' Creed

As necromancers, we reach into people's souls and awaken all that they have been. As necroturgists, we point that awakened awareness toward the future and what may be done in the present to create that future. We give birth to our ancestors and the world dances on.

Some people are waiting to live and others are waiting to die, but we elfin have given up waiting.

The end of the world lies on the border of Eternity.

Old Elven Sayings About Money, Gold, and Wealth

❧

"AN EMPTY PURSE BENEFITS NO ONE." . . . . .

The Power of Wealth is sharing.

Elves seldom value things in financial terms, an object made of gold would be valued for its beauty. Lacking that, no amount of money could persuade them it is something of true worth.

Great wealth should not impoverish others, but enrich them; otherwise it will in time itself become greatly impoverished.

It is rumored among men that we elfin can temporarily turn stones and leaves into gold. They call it faery gold, and shortly after it is received, it returns to its true shape. In truth, to elfin eyes and for those enchanted by Faerie, everything glitters with magic. It is hardly our fault that to us a stone or a leaf seems more beautiful and valuable than a piece of printed paper that men call money.

The rich often feel that those who are less wealthy are beneath them but they should remember that the Earth, who supports us all and from whom nearly all wealth comes, is beneath them as well.

The difference between elves and men may be chiefly this, that men crave money and power and are ever seeking to control people, while we elves yearn for love and friendship and are ever seeking to set souls free.

If you long for love, give it. If you yearn for beauty, create it. If you desire wealth, share it. Such are the secrets of the Elven Way. —Zaradon the Wyzard

Some people will do anything for money. But to elves, money is merely a tool rather like toilet paper.

For many folks, the most difficult thing to understand about elfin culture is our belief that by sharing the little you have, you'll have even more.

Gold comes with the smile of the Divine and the grin of the Wicked.

Sayings About Elfin Children, Education and Learning

"WE ELVES HAVE NOTICED THAT THE MOST VOCAL EXPERTS ON RAISING CHILDREN ARE ALWAYS THOSE WHO'VE NEVER HAD ANY OF THEIR OWN." .
. . . .

Never pass up an opportunity to learn. —Old Elven Saying

"You need to raise your children from the very first preparing for the day when they will leave you and go out on their own. And if you can do that so your time together is filled with happiness then you can be certain that they shall be happy thereafter and in their happiness lives your own." ....By Myloryn — Advice to Parents

We elves believe in education the same as we believe in life. It goes on forever.

We elves seldom spoil our children, but we do let them ripe pretty thoroughly.

They say that those that can do and those that can't teach. Yet we elves teach by doing, lead by example and learn from all we do.

Elves seldom speak of punishment or retribution but rather of balance, healing, and fairness.

The elves say a good education lubricates the mind so all one's prejudices and preconceptions slip out and away.

Mankind and others less Kind often tell us they attend the school of hard knocks. While we elves have occasionally taken classes there, we much prefer our own Universities of Lucky Breaks.

Telling little children there is no Santa Claus is like ripping the wings off Faeries. Santa doesn't mind if you don't believe in him but crushing the magic in children really pisses him off.

"You can't force wisdom to come; you can just embrace it when it does."
—Old Elven Saying

"LEARNING IS NOT A COLLECTION OF FACTS BUT AN ACCUMULATION OF EXPERIENCES." . . . . .

We always let our children know that whenever they encounter someone who wants them to conform to a particular style of dress or belief without question that they are being led astray from Elfin, where one is always encouraged to think for ones'elf and to create one's own style.

We elves don't try to force our children to be anything in particular. We simply encourage them to always do their best at being thems'elves.

Elves are profound believers in the powers of reason. Thus, whenever we ask a child to do something and sHe asks "why?" we don't say "Because I said so," but rather we explain the reasons for our request.

Normal folk do not understand how we elves teach our children if we explain it to them and cannot see it when demonstrated. So we simply leave them to suppose, quite falsely, that we teach as they do, which is a lesson in itself though they are loath to learn it.

The elves do not divide the world between those who are smart and those who are stupid but between those who are eager to learn and those too ignorant to realize their need to do so.

"One should always embrace an opportunity to learn." —Old Elven Saying

Elves don't except unthinking obedience but rather thoughtful questions.

When elven children are naughty their parents never tell them the boogey man will get them. Instead, we tell them that if they continue being naughty they may wind up being normal folk, which is a thought that most elves find terrifying.

To the elves, education is never a competition between people but always a competition with ones'elf.

Elves equate life with education, for they ever strive to learn.

To the Elfin, education and entertainment are the same thing.

"TO THE ELFIN MIND, CHILDREN CAN DO NOTHING WRONG THAT THEY HAVE NOT LEARNED FROM THEIR PARENTS.". . . . .

Men are always telling their children to grow up. We are always telling ours to have fun.

We elves though we are often high born are ever on the side of the lowly, though we are cultured and refined we appreciate the simple and sincere; and though we tend to be educated, we encourage those who strive to learn. No matter who a person is, we ever seek to lift them up and encourage them.

If you wish to raise individuals to live in a free society, you must encourage them to be free spirits, which means not merely urging them to accept responsibility for their own decisions but also allowing them to make those decisions.

There is a Goddess in every Woman, a God in every Man, and an Elf in every Child or is that a Child in every Elf?

We elves think education should be like a game that is fun and exciting to play.

It is easier and, in the long run, quicker to do things correctly the first time, although not always as educational.

Elves never teach; they share.

It is the nature of elves to influence people using psychology and moral rectitude rather than violence and intimidation. They appeal to the best in people while understanding the worse. They uplift the soul and the spirit of others while tempering their own and thus set a clear example for all to learn by.

Every child in Elfin is raised to be a princess or a prince, to achieve greatness, to fulfill thems'elves completely each hir own unique way.

We elves don't teach our children so much as provide them with everything they need in order to learn.

Elves are simultaneously the most childlike and mature individuals in the world, which is confusing to adults but makes perfect sense to children.

Elfin Wisdom About Love and Happiness, Friendship and Kindness, Romance and Relationships

"WE ELVES OFTEN REFER TO ROMANCE AS SHARING DREAMS." . . . .

Men sometimes say that Time is of the Essence. We elves say that Love is the Essence and Time the means of manifesting it.

"Relationships are a tapesty woven from star light." Ancient Elven Knowledge.

There is within us a longing that we elves are ever subjected to, except in those all too brief moments when we lay embracing, naked in each other's arms.

People do not have to reciprocate our love for we elves to love them, but it is absolutely vital that they pass it on.

For most people, history is the story of what battles and wars they've lost and won and the heroes there of. For we Elfin, history is the tale of the music we've composed, the literature we've written and the art we've created, and the lovers who inspired it all.

The material world was born of a romance between the light and the dark. Like every relationship, there are things to work out.

It is the Destiny of elves to create Elfin and to bring it to life with our love.

If you ask an elf what god or goddess is their favorite, we nearly always say, the one we're making love to at the moment.

We've heard it said that men do strange things for love; Elves do all things for love.

Love knows no boundaries of its own,
While never violating those set by others. —Old Elven Saying

"In our hearts and in our minds our love forever is entwined now and forever more, we'll meet again on further shore." —Ancient Elven Love Song

"THE HEROES OF MAN ARE POLITICIANS, WARRIORS, AND SPORTS FIGURES; THE HEROES OF ELVES ARE ARTISTS, INVENTORS, AND GREAT LOVERS." . . . . .

We elves do not worship the gods so much as romance them.

If someone rejects you, thank them. They have helped you more than you realize.

The elves are under the opinion that people who reject us are usually doing us a favor.

There are those among occultist who speak of Storming the gates of Heaven and taking them by force. This is not true of Elfin. One cannot force their way into Elfin any more than we can compel someone to love us. Elfin bestows its favours when it will and we can but make ours'elves ready by becoming worthy and suitable lovers.

We elves have no fixed limits on how many lovers or husbands or wives a person can have either sequentially or if you must tread the hidden paths at night, at least do it beneath the moon and stars.

"Friendship is built with a thousand hellos." —Old Elven Saying

The Elfin say: "Kindness is older than Time."

The Elves say: "Elfin is never further than a trusted friend."

The voice of Faerie echoes in every heart that yearns for Love.

We elves don't believe in tough love, but rather gentle discipline.

In spite of what some have written, we elves seldom drink alcoholic beverages. For us there are few things more intoxicating than love.

Elves come together and separate as easily as water, save we ever carry the memory of our union in our hearts.

If we elves could have what we really want, what we'd have is... you.

"THE SOURCE OF ALL THINGS IS LOVE. WHEREVER YOU FIND LOVE, THERE YOU WILL FIND THE MAGIC BEING BORN." . . . . .

Happiness is the great panacea.

The greatest ambition of most elves is to live together in love, peace, and harmony.

They say love makes the world go around. Thus the elves use love to create magic and magic to create love and in this way keep the great dance spinning.

Love begins with friendship and resides there as well.

If the Elves had our way, we'd be friends with everyone.
That some folk choose not to be our friends is eternally a mystery to us,
for they do not realize the wonders they are missing out on.

Most people say, "You only have one life to live."
Elves say. "You only have one life to live at a time, so do your best with each one,"
which is also how we approach relationships.

Elves consider love and kindness to be types of intelligence. The more loving and kind you are the more intelligent you're considered. Those who are kind and loving to everyone they meet, are thought to be geniuses.

Love is sometimes hard. Often needs to be firm. But is never tough.

Cleverness is greatly appreciated by we elfin but not valued nearly as much as kindness and sincerity.

Happiness isn't something we find or something that happens to us or arrives as a gift, it's a choice we make.

"Happiness is a decision you make about life." —Old Elfin Saying

Elfin Saying: Most people seek Love, Elves create it.

Vampires are made immortal through the blood of a vampire. Elves are made immortal through the love of an elf.

"ELVES TEND TO THINK WITH OUR FEELINGS AND FEEL WITH OUR MINDS; THUS WE MAKE DECISIONS FROM OUR GUT AND CARESS WITH OUR EYES.".

. . . .

We elves do sometimes laugh at people's foibles but not in cruel disregard of them but in deepest affection.

When we find someone who is particularly kind and understanding, we elves tend to think of them as elven. There are those who would object to this, saying that kindness and understanding are not traits that are exclusive to the elves... which is true. Yet these are such salient aspects of the elfin character that to us, anyone who strongly demonstrates these characteristics is accepted by us as one of our own.

Some people seem to think that the return of Elfin would be the end for cars and computers. However, the appearance of Elfin does not depend on the presence or absence of technology, but the presence or absence of love and kindness.

There are only two ways to love among the elven: fully and completely.

Trust is so important to the Elven that those who violate our trust are treated as though they never existed, which as they fade from our lives becomes reality.

Elves are a deeply sensual people and have a great and abiding interest in sexuality, yet we place but small emphasis upon differences of gender.

It is said that the way to a man's heart is through his stomach. If so, the way to an Elfin heart is through our fingertips.

There are certain people who for some curious reason seem to enjoy 'jerking each other's chains.' We elfin prefer to tickle each other's fancy.

"The more you share, the more you have. Some share misery, others share love."
—The Wisdom of the Elves

If you are looking for Faerie, look upon the faces of the Fae.

When elves marry we don't say "till death do us part" but rather "friends forever."

True love makes everyone more elfin.

On Living the Elven Myth

"SOME PEOPLE SAY, 'FAKE IT TILL YOU MAKE IT', BUT WE ELVES SAY, 'BE IT UNTIL YOU BECOME IT'. . . . .

Some people say we elves are creatures of myth and we agree. We elves are indeed mythic beings, which ordinary mortals do well to remember.

Shakespeare wrote that all the world is a play and all of us players, and in that he was surely fey touched, for this is the elfin view of reality: "All is as we make it, rather than fixed eternally beforehand."

As Above, So Below,
As Within, So Without,
What goes around, Comes Around,
And we elves sit in the center
And watch with fascination.

"Some individuals try to make fun of the elves but nearly always fail, ending up frustrated and angry while we go merrily on our way, smiling all the while." —from the archives of elven history

When the Fae are about to go exploring, we often express this by saying we are off to do wild things in strange places.

We've often heard people say, "What you see is what you get." With the elves, what you see is just the wrapping.

We elves are always on time, — our time.

It's true we elves get small support in most societies for choosing to be who we really are; yet if we did not choose to be ourselves, who else would ever dare to be elves.

Elves say: "All of life is an adventure, which is why it is so often difficult and dangerous. We will surely fall in time, but if we proceed with courage we shall be remembered as heroes."

"An arrow without fletchings seldom hits the target."
— Olde Elven Saying meaning: A person without a family
and friends to guide hir is unlikely to succeed.

Elven Sayings on Elfin Kin, Family and Kinship

ॐ

"THERE IS SOMETHING IN EACH ELFIN HEART THAT WILL NEVER BE FULFILLED UNTIL ALL OUR PEOPLES ARE UNITED AND HAPPY.". . . .

For most elves, memories of Elfin are not so much thoughts or images but feelings of kinship that wash over our beings like music.

Even when we've never met previously, elves nearly always recognize each other. It is not that we remember with our minds so much as our hearts.

We elfin do not understand the concept of Kings and Queens as it is perceived by most folk. To we elves, a king is someone who donates everything they have for the sake of the people. So you must be very careful of what you claim around the elven or we will be showing up at your door continually, expecting to be invited to dinner.

We elves are like magnets; we draw others of our kind to us wherever we go.

Elves know ours'elves to be kin to all faerie kind. We nurture the best in each and all.

Elves consider thems'elves family. From group, clan, tribe to nation, all are kin.

Some suspect we are a cult seeking converts. In truth, we are elves seeking our family, friends, and lovers.

The memories of the elves are stored not just in our minds but in our hearts as well.

When elves say good night to kin, they speak of dream time and say, "We shall see you, dear kin, Upon the Wing.

Everyone has a place in Elfin and each is respected whatever hir (his/her) place. It does not matter if one's place seems high or low, all are equal in the heart of the elven magic and in their faerie kindreth.

Faerie folk bring color to a drab and dreary world.

When men ask us who wears the pants in our family, we elves reply: We all do.

"Water Runs If You Try To Grasp It,
But Pours Onto An Open Hand."
—Old Elven Riddle

Ancient Elven Expressions, Koans and Riddles

"A NEW DAY ALWAYS BEGINS IN DARKNESS.". . . . .

A world composed only of Elven is not an Elfin world at all.

The riddle of life is death. The riddle of death is life. The answer to life's riddle is eternal change. The answer to death's riddle is everlasting bliss.

The quickest way to Elfin is being there.

The world is as real as we make it.

It is said that the early bird catches the worm, which is fine by the elves since we have little interest in worms.

There are those who complain that we elves contradict ourselves. But can the left hand contradict the right? The nature of life is paradoxical, so how can we speak the truth without speaking to all sides of a question?

There is no satisfaction without longing.

The elves are under the impression that the Book of Job is about being forced to work for a living.

The past can only be altered through the present.

"Nothing lasts forever, everything always is." —Elven Koan

The elves say that in the end it comes down to this,
"A New Beginning!" —Elven Riddle

Live a little. Love a lot!

"FROM THE SAME CLAY, WE ARE ALL MADE UNIQUE." —ANCIENT ELVEN RIDDLE. . . . . .

The more you know about Life the more it surprises you.

"I am me to me and you to you, while you are me to you and you to me." —Old Elven Koan … Note: We can see why toddlers scream on trying to learn this language. They call this the terrible twos—they got that right, you and me.

If the path of life was always smooth we'd slip and fall.

The elves believe the more we share, the more we have.

The elves say that for most people the end of the road is the beginning of the path.

"The more we find Elfin within us, the more it begins to appear all about us." —Elven Koan

"The typical elf isn't." —Elven Koan

The closer we come to being our true s'elves, the easier we find each other.

Things are the way they are, but they can be whatever we wish them to be.

Unfortunately, those who seem to need us most seem to want us least.

Elven Proverb: "Enjoying the game is the best way to win."

We elves frequently count on Fantasy stories to keep us in touch with reality.

Elven Koan: "People don't become elves, elves are people who become."

Life is a puzzle. Our job is to fit the right pieces together so we can see the bigger picture.

The truth is simply complicated.

What the Elves Say About Evolution

"THE ELVES SAY: "EVEN THE MYTHS EVOLVE!" . . . . .

Evolution is like a relay race, we carry the baton of wisdom, power, and knowledge to those awaiting us in the future.
—Ancient Elven Knowledge

Some people may wonder why if we could live in Faerie, would we bother to live in this world. But we elves see Faerie being born all around us.

The landscape of faerie is ever changing like the shifting sands of a desert.

It is not so much that the elves will come back to save the Earth and humanity, so much as humanity must become more elven to save itself and the Earth.

By transforming ours'elves, we change everything.

If you read fantasy books about us, one might get the idea that we elves hate orcs, goblins and others of their kind but we do not. We ever wish them healing, enlightenment and evolutionary development. In the meantime, however, we may have to fill them with arrows to let the light in.

We elves have also evolved through mineral and animal lifetimes, although it is true we were elven crystals and elfin foxes, wolves and porpoises.

Every day in Faerie is a new day, the same day, the Eternal day, forever changing.

Caterpillars transform into Butterflies. But what do Butterflies evolve into? ... Faeries?

Every mother gives birth to worlds. —Elven Saying

Elven Words To Live By

"KNOWLEDGE IS ACHIEVED BY THE MIND. WISDOM IS BORN FROM THE HEART AND GUT." . . . .

If you're not in touch with your own heart, you can't really touch anyone else's.

There are those who think that we elfin are destined to be the Rulers of the Earth. But that is of no interest to us. As far as we can see, Rulers spend most of their time measuring things. To say one is the Ruler is to say they are the Head Clerk. What sort of ambition is that?

Mere words do not wash one's actions clear.

It is easier to be something than believe you are something; therefore, do and be and allow belief to come in its own time.

Some folks claim the waters of Elfin are intoxicating. Others say it is the air or the fragance of the flowers, the food, the drink... which is all true. But the most intoxicating thing about Elfin really, is the elves and the love we share.

We elfin think that the only true fool is the one that doesn't admit it.

Sometimes folks approach the elfin as though we know the answers to all of life's questions. We surely do not. Infact, we very much doubt we know all the questions.

Some folks are looking for adventure. We elves see it everywhere.

When elves say, "Life is change," They mean it quite literally.

Often when we encounter people, they return our smiles with looks of suspicion. We cannot but help feel the most incredible compassion for these folks.

The elfin frequently bend over backwards to help others in need. We believe stretching to be therapeutic.

"THE EASIEST WAY TO GET PEOPLE TO CHANGE IS TO ACCEPT THEM AS THEY ARE." . . . . .

It is unwise and futile to attempt to deny a fool their right to suffer. It is generally confusing and disturbing if you awaken a sleepwalker. So one is ever counseled to lead them back to bed and allow them to awaken in their own time. It is for this reason as well that we do not attempt to disturb those elves who have as yet not awakened to their true natures. We simply sing softly as they sleep and know that in time they will come to realize that we are more than just a dream.

We are told that the idea of good creates the idea of evil and vice versa. We elves do not deny that this is true intellectually. But good's proper place is in Being and evil's place is best found in non-being. Thus when we pursue our true course and Will in life, all things fall into their proper place.

We elves define architecture as the science of building in harmony with nature and the art of contributing to the elegance of the soul.

There are times when all we see before us is a vast and empty wasteland. And we could despair to see such longing and desperation. But instead we bend and plant the seeds of hope and possibility and love from which shimmering trees of magic shall grow.

The Elfin believe that secrets can never really be revealed in books but they can be hinted at.

When the wind comes howling over the hilltops the Elfin often observe, "They're coming."

The Elven say: "If you have to think about it, you don't know."

The Elven say: "Advice unsought is seldom heeded."

The elfin say: There are those who speak as though they were wise and those whose lives speak for them.

Intolerance is un-elfin, except of intolerance for the intolerant.

"WISDOM NOT ACTED UPON IS A TREE THAT BEARS NO FRUIT." . . . . .

"Life is by its nature symbiotic. We can only succeed together." —The Wisdom of the Elves.

Wise Elves know: "There's no larger detour sign than pain."

If you wish to know the truth about someone, listen carefully about what they say about you.

In stories and in life, power is often shared in some object, like a ring or signet of a king, or an amulet or some symbol of office and authority. Such powers, however, always reside within the "office" itself and belongs to the individual only so long as they have the "ring" or symbol of authority in their possession. We elves seek not such power but instead to develop the powers that live in potential within our own being so that whether we are king or janitor, we will accomplish that office with the full power of a vibrant personality and soul.

The elves are of the opinion that the sun gets up far too early in the morning. We'd never tell him that, but we do try to set a better example.

Simplifying one's life is like doing dishes, even when you've washed them all they're never done.

"The truth may be painful, but the failure to face the truth may kill you."
—Old Elven Words to Live Well By

The ethics of Elfin are simple: in all things do what is fair.

There are many folk who have a passion for revenge. They cannot be at peace until they have righted an injustice. The Elfin have a similar passion to repay those who have done us some great kindness. Of course, we are not beyond revenge, but are often more patience in its fulfillment, content, most often, to let time and nature do our work for us.

No one goes hungry in Elfin and yet the elves seldom tend to be over weight. There is a lesson in this somewhere.

You can't cure another's illness by catching it.

THE ELFIN SAY: "WISDOM CAN BE FOUND IN THE MEADOW AS WELL AS ON THE MOUNTAIN TOP." . . . . .

Some tales say that one should never thank the fae. We elves find this a curious idea since we are quite big on courtesy. It is true that one should be sincere in thanking us, but even then if an insincere "Thanks" ultimately leads one to learn better manners, we are all for it.

Be kind to those who are less intelligent for if it wasn't for them we wouldn't seem so very smart.

The Elven say: "Compromise is greater than victory and longer lasting."

The Elfin say: "On occasion an ill deed can be left to go unpunished, for people often do ill unintentionally and their own guilt is punishment enough. But a good deed should never go unrewarded, even when done for the wrong reasons; good should always be encouraged."

Usually when a can of worms gets opened, it's a sign that it's time to go fishing.

You cannot create peace by force.

Truth is best when it becomes one's friend and not merely an acquaintance. One needs to know it well and embrace it and be loyal ever after.

The quickest way to find Faerie is to be faerie.

"Putting a beautiful spread on a lumpy bed doesn't make it comfortable to sleep on but it is still lovely to look at." —What the Elves Say

When two or more are gathered in the name of Faerie, something wondrous is bound to occur.

The Universe is not a stagnant structure but a living being and thus we are wise to be ever adaptable in encountering it.

The true Nature of the Universe is infinite possibility.
You are just one of its many fabulous ideas.

"The Shining Ones say we are droplets of fire in an Ocean of Light."
—Ancient Elven Wisdom

Ancient Elven Wisdom about the Shining Ones and the Divine Spirit

"Some people think the Shining Ones are part of a vast conspiracy. They are. It's called Evolution!" . . . . .

The Shining Ones exist throughout the Universe, weaving starlight to uplift all.

The Breath of the Spirit fills our lungs.

The more we become like the Shinning Ones, the more we tend to glow.

The Elfin are somewhat confused by church goers, for the Elves believe we are closer to the Divine when we create than when we pray.

The Shining Ones are surely greater than us, more powerful and more evolved and yet in the end they are still family and that is more important than anything.

When the Elven speak of spirit they are not talking of spiritual so much as spirited.

Spirit is the fire that warms the soul. The Elvish say the Divine sees the beauty of every soul.

The Divine expresses itself through Nature. In becoming one with Nature, we become one with the Divine.

Many folk see elves as very high spiritual beings
And surely spirit is of great interest to us,
But such folk should remember that
We see the very Earth as Divine.

Many find it hard to understand but the elfin, even when they seem to be having the most frivolous of moments, hold a still point of reverence in their hearts for the Divine in all its manifestations. It is a mystery, but even in laughter the elfin hold purpose.

Why do the Shining Ones care? Is it that we are so important? Well, we are important to them as a child is dear to its parents, as a lover to its beloved, as a family is to each other. They care because we are theirs and they ours. It is as simple and wondrous as that.

To the elves, the cartoon image of a light bulb going on over a person's head when they have a sudden idea is a fairly good allegory of the beginning of the Universe.

There are those who think the elves are touched, which may be true, for the Divine has molded us with Hir very own Hands.

Ancient Elven Knowledge About the Shining Ones:
From our birth to our death, they guide us and every choice we make is another lesson of life and magic. From our death to our birth, they carry us, like a wave washing us to shore and a new incarnation.

The Shining Ones guide all who call to them and many who know not of their existence but are of good heart and striving spirit.

The Shining Ones are not Gods, although some may think them so for they are great and powerful.

The Shining Ones know us better than anyone. Thus, those who trust them and those who don't usually have good reasons for doing so.

While the Shining Ones guide us, they do not compel. The choice is ever ours and they would not interfere with our magic.

The Shining Ones don't have auras, they are auras.

To serve the Shining Ones is to become one of them, for their lives are a continuing example of service.

The spiritual quest for the elves is not religious in nature but energetic. We seek to prefect ours'elves and to become the best we can be.

"WE CALL THEM SHINING ONES BECAUSE THEY GLOW. THEY ARE STARS —
BEINGS OF LIGHT.". . . . .

People claim that we elfin are a product of someone's imagination. We don't deny this. We merely wish to point out that, that someone is Divine.

The Shining Ones say we should try to make each day a little bit brighter. We do not aspire to be Shining Ones, but to be our own true s'elves and on achieving that, we become ever more beings of light.

You can describe the relationship between the elves and the Shining Ones as being spiritual but it would be more accurate to describe it as affectionate.

Some think the Shining Ones are dragons and there is surely a poetic truth in that.

We elves do not look upon the Shining Ones as Gods or even as our bosses, but as those whose every act of being inspires us.

You could think of the Shining Ones as teachers. But if they teach, it is by example only.

If you are looking for the Keys to the higher dimensions, the Shining Ones are those Keys.

The Shining Ones are eager to aid and assist us, but they will never help us to do those things that do not ultimately benefit our spiritual and evolutionary development.

The Shining Ones are more varied than the trees and more populous than the stars.

The Shinning Ones see the fact that many people lie to make themselves seem better than they are reveals their inner hunger to evolve.

The more we become like the Shinning Ones, the more we tend to glow.

Spirit is the fire that warms the soul.

The Divine is not deceived by empty flattery.

The Shining Ones say the First Cause is our desire to be whole.

The Shining Ones live among the stars but they also live among the trees of the forest, the rocks of the high mountains and the waves of the ocean deep.

The Shining Ones say we will always find those who are meant for us if we trust our natural attractions.

The Shining Ones are not demons one can control or order about. They are more like an eccentric relative one has invited to visit but who unexpectedly shows up on one's doorstep with a twinkle in their eyes and a knowing smile on their lips.

The Shining Ones are not your parents, your aunt, uncle, cousins, brother, sister; but they very well may have been so in previous lifetimes.

The Shining Ones can not be coerced, bribed, or commanded. They are, however, swayed by enchantment, which is what the elves are ever about.

The Shining Ones do not reward us for doing good deeds or punish those who are bad*, but favor those who live life with spirit, elegance and style.
* that is the work of the Lords of Karma

We are not defined by the Spirits that assist us, but our nature's attract those who are meant for us.

The Shinning Ones ever wish the best for us and they fulfill that wish by helping us become the very best we can be.

It is said of the Shining Ones that their coming is like small stars gliding through the forest.

The Shinning Ones say that at the end of the Universe, we will all take a bow. And the elves will throw the cast party!

Elf Quotes About Elfin Runes, Tarot and Other Oracles

"OF ALL THE ORACLES PERHAPS THE GREATEST IS OUR OWN DREAMS." . . .
. .

We elfin often blow on our runes and chant or hum or sing while casting the stones in order to unite them with the Breath of Life and the Song of Creation.

Most folks seem to think of Runes as Magical letters or glyphs but the Elfin understand these sigils to be merely symbols for the sounds by which the Universe is created.

If you ask the Fae what our favorite archtectual buildings of man are, we most often answer, "Ancient Ruins."

The Elves often refer to the tarot as a Living Book or a Book of Life for like life it evolves and changes from day to day.

The Elves often refer to the tarot cards as leaves. This is thought to be because they originally used leaves from the trees or perhaps bark.

For the elven, the tarot cards represent magical powers and can not only be used as symbolic communication with the spirits but can also be combined to create various spells and formulas and cantrips.

Some Elves say it was they who taught the Druids the language of the trees, a leaf from each tree being used like a tarot card for prophecy and communication.

 Fate is a line on the hand of Destiny.

If you ask the elves to look into the future, they will tell you there is no future, there is only nearly infinite possibility.

Elven seers don't so much look into the future as look at the possibilities.

"Faerie is just around the corner, over the hill,
around the bend, and right where you are standing."
—What the Elven Say

What the Elven Say About Awakening to Faerie

❧

"A SONG CONSTANTLY PLAYS IN THE ELVEN SOUL. ITS MELODY IS THE CALL OF ADVENTURE AND ITS HARMONY IS THE CALL OF FAERIE." . . . . .

When elves first awaken to the realization of who they really are, there is often a euphoria that sets in but this enchantment only ever lasts for a short while and then grounded once more the individual is faced with the fact that magic, even elfin magic, requires effort and a decision to go on.

Men say life is an eternal struggle between good and evil, whereas elves see life as a continuous struggle to awaken.

What do elves seek in the world? We seek to awaken the magic in all we encounter.

Elves do not seek to make waves in the world. The fact that some folks are surprised, even shocked, to see us says more about them than us. Yet to our minds, the fact that they see us at all is a good sign that humanity is Awakening.

The light of Faerie is an inner light, it shines not on our faces so much as it illuminates our hearts and minds.

We may at times leave Faerie, but Faerie never leaves us.

The elves will tell you, "Everything is alive in Faerie!" And if you reply, "Well, every thing is alive on earth," They will say, "Exactly so."

Each person who comes to Faerie from the mundane world struggles to adapt to the inevitable changes. If they embrace these changes they go deeper. But if the changes prove too much for them, they flee—cast out from the wonder they could not endure.

"The more we awaken, the brighter we become in all ways." —What the Elves Know

Beginning to see Faerie is much like letting one's eyes adjust to the dark. Once one does, one finds that what at first seemed hidden becomes quite visible.

"FAERIE BELONGS TO EACH AND ALL OF US.
IT GIVES BIRTH TO US IN SPIRIT AS WE GIVE BIRTH TO IT IN REALITY.
LIKE US, IT WEARS MANY FACES AND YET REMAINS EVER SAME IN ITS EVER CHANGING NATURE.". . . . .

Trying to control Faerie is like repressing one's true nature.
Sooner or later its latent power grown strong through restriction will burst free.

Most people are ever awaiting the One who will come and save the world. The elves are ever seeking to awaken the many.

If you wish to enter Faerie it is important to understand that your body is already there, it is your perception that needs to cross the threshold.

When one enters Faerie, they realize they have been there forever.

We've heard Faerie compared to a mirage that keeps getting further away or disappears altogether when one seems to get close to it. But really Faerie is like a parent with their arms outstretched crouching just beyond reach as their toddler takes its first hesitant steps.

You may wander through Faerie forever and never see it all because it is ever changing.

For Faerie kind, all paths lead to Faerie.

Some folks insist on Faerie being a dangerous place and for them, it is. For Faerie fulfills our deepest wishes, while astounding our assumptions and exceeding our expectations.

If you are seeking Faerie, it is here. It always has been, it ever will be.

The deeper you go into Faerie, the more amazing it becomes.

Faerie doesn't create we elves and other fae folk so much as allow us a place to be who we really are.

Every step toward Faerie brings one closer and closer to one's true s'elf.

"WHEN YOU FIND FAERIE, EVEN A BIT OF IT, HANG ON AND NEVER LET IT GO.". . . . .

At the ends of the Earth, you find Faerie.

Some people say that Faerie smells like sunshine, others say its like an ocean breeze, others still, like the air after the rain, and some that it is like fresh brewed coffee or home baked bread and some even that it is like the smell of sex after hours of love making. They are all correct.

If you ask an elf where you might find Faerie, the elf will likely point to your heart.

You can spend lifetimes in Faerie and still be amazed.

Faerie is vast, yet there is no part that does not touch another.

It is common for the newly awakened elfin to assume that all elves are like them, but in time we come to realize that mainly what we share in common is our uniqueness.

Faerie doesn't just await us. It's ever searching.

Faerie is born of the love between the Spirit and the Soul.

There is always at least a little bit of fae blood in those who yearn for Faerie, those who are fascinated by Faerie and those who see a glimpse of faerie. These are ever of faerie kind.

Faerie is ever changing, because everyday we create it anew.

Contrary to what most folks think, Faerie is ever ready to embrace you. You just need to reach out.

Faerie is like a wonderful dream you awaken from only to discover it has come true.

Not everyone who seeks Faerie, finds Faerie, but Faerie finds all who truly love her.

Faerie arrives at the moment when we stop waiting for it and start creating it.

Elves Speak About Dreams and Visions

"Dreams are our soul's way of speaking with our spirit.". . . . .

What is death but another dream?

Meditation, astral travel and lucid dreaming are the third step to making our dreams reality. The second step is living the dream and the first, loving with all your heart.

If you look to others to tell you what your dreams should be, you'll wind up living other people's dreams.

Ver Aleli Vasadas (in Arvyndase, language of the Silver Elves, "In dreams awakening").

The dream world and what most people call reality are one and the same to the elves, just different parts of one reality, which is in its'elf a dream. It is in this way that we have the power to make dreams become real.

The Elves not only have dream catchers in their homes, but also dream liberators as well.

There are folks who believe that we elfin exist only on the etheric and astral planes. Others say we exist only on the mental planes as constructs of imagination. But the truth is we exist on all planes of being and help guide and communicate with each other through our dreams, visions, and aspirations.

Elf Saying: "Dreams are our connection to infinite possibility."

Faerie is little more than a dream made real by magic, and yet that is nearly everything."

We elves define an optimist as someone with such good eyesight that they are able to see through the mists of doubt and illusion to the radiance of Living Elfin that awaits beyond and in our dreams.

Stepping into Faerie is like waking from a dream and realizing you're still dreaming.

"WE DREAM OF FAERIE BUT FAERIE ALSO DREAMS OF US." . . . . .

We elves define an optimist as someone
With such good eyesight that they are able to see
Through the mists of doubt and illusion
To the radiance of Living Elfin
That awaits beyond, and in our dreams.

So many authors write about elves as though we were their nightmares,
When we would rather be their dreams come true.

We know when we draw near to Elfin for we feel as though we're in a dream.
Elfin is not so much Lucid Dreaming as Dreaming Lucidly.

You could say that all of life is a vision quest for the elfin, although it's probably
more accurate to say that for us all of life is a vision.

Faerie is closer to waking consciousness than a dream and closer to a dream than
waking consciousness. It is like an adventure, a journey or a trip ... in which
everything is new and time seems almost suspended.

Enchantment not only makes dreams come true, it also sets us dreaming.

There are three things elves cherish: those we love, those who love us, and those we
will come to love.

Enchantment is a curious magic because it comes naturally and yet is learned,
mostly by learning to be natural.

Elven Bumper Stickers and Grafetti

"MEN RULE! ELVES LIBERATE!" . . . . .

Many stars, one sky.

Calm and patience achieve what haste and hurry delay.

Jesus saves, Buddha recycles, the elves dumpster dive.

Luck shared is luck multiplied.

Wait not on inspiration, act upon it!

The secret to life is "Yes."

There are no exceptions to
The rules in Elfin,
There are also
No rules.

The Elfin read between the lines but also beyond them.

If you want to keep your "head straight" you need to keep your eyes on the goal."

The best disguise is other people's!

Elf Means Friend!

Elves don't keep pets, we keep friends.

"May the Day Come to us."
—Wisdom remembered by our eldar sister Arwen of the Elf Queen's Daughters

Most people say, "Shit happens." The Elves exclaim, "Free fertilizer."

"WE ARE ONE, TOGETHER AND ALONE." . . . . .

Elven expression: "Make it fun!"

We elves tend to be very traditional and conservative in a very radical and liberal way.

Love is Magic, Magic is Love!

The Call of Faerie is the echo of our heart's desire.

Lady Luck is an elf.

People don't become elves, elves are people who become.

"We're Elves! What in Middle Earth are you?"
—An Elven Bumper Sticker

Faeries don't litter, they glitter!

Faerie is a memory of our future.

"Why Not?"
—Old Elven Saying

We elves don't get jet lagged, we get time warped.

"Healing is contageous! Pass it around."
—Old Elven Saying

Enchantment dances,
Enchantment sings,
Enchantment gives the faeries wings!

Elfin Knowledge on Creativity, Art and Imagination

"THE ELVES ARE NEARLY ALWAYS CREATING SOMETHING, USUALLY FUN." .
. . . .

Reason Speaks of what is. Imagination whispers what could be!

Thoughts exist in an ocean of mind. When we elves seek inspiration, we go swimming in our imaginations.

While most people are busy trying to make it in the world, the elves are busy creating it.

To the elves, creativity and magic are the same.

If you ask the elves if they prefer poetry or prose, they will tell you they love whatever piques their interests and arouses their imagination.

Elves say that poetry and fiction often reveal truths that are currently beyond the grasp of non-fiction and science.

To elves, poetry is a way of speaking about mysteries that words alone can never unravel.

The elves say:
"Life is about change. Life is change. Life is about love and creativity."

Whatever elves do in the world, whether it be accounting or auto-mechanics, they always consider themselves artists.

If you wish to enter Faerie, you need to develop your powers of imagination.
If you wish to be safe in Faerie, you need to develop tranquility of Soul.

The Elven imagination shapes the mists of Faerie into magic.

Elves decorate the world with their imagination and a most wondrous world it is.

Elves don't get bored; we get creative.

We elves don't practice magic; we perform it.

There is no open, free-flowing, artistic, creative place, gathering or situation that a little bureaucracy can't foul up. —Elven Saying

"We elves see faces in the clouds, in the trees, in the stones ... this is not just our imagination but an understanding of the magical nature of reality."

"All true education begins with imagination."

Elves define nearly everything as art: dancing is art, writing is art, auto mechanics if done with excellence and a bit of panache is considered art. But one of the greatest arts of all is living with style.

The key to the portal to Faerie is your own imagination made real through your life.

The key to the portal to Faerie is imagination, not because Faerie isn't real but because creativity is at the heart of Faerie.

Faerie grows in a fertile imagination like seeds sprout in rich soil.

To the elves, all of life is a canvas for our arts.

Beauty is a magic that we speak of with ease but is often the result of great effort as though the artist has climbed up a high mountain and now rests at its peak enjoying the magnificent view.

Elves consider all art to be spells of enchantment cast to transform the world.

"Just as a tree roots are hidden beneath the earth,
the roots of Magic are obscured by the invisible"
—Hidden Knowledge of the Elven Magicians

Wisdom Spoken By Elves About The Unseen And The Unknown

"Certain mystics say that you can only see the fae by looking unfocused from the corners of your eye. We elves say that we can't be seen unless one focuses on the center of their heart." . . . . . .

The Elvish say the Beginning of all things is in the Unseen.

The Elvish say: "Many become famous, most are forgotten but those who shape the world go unnamed."

"There is a difference between the unknown and the unknowable. One exists and the other doesn't." Elfin Saying.

Most people think that Elfin is only a fantasy. They are half right. It is a realm of Fantasy, but not only.

The elven see the truth hidden in all things, even falsehood.

The reason we are invisible to most folks is not because we are hiding but because they refuse to see.

Elves ever live on the border between the Known and the Yet to be Discovered.

Life is filled with the unexpected possibilities, although often they are hiding, waiting for someone to pass by so they can pop out and yell, "Surprise!"

As we breath deep, we settle into that place of elfish magic where the energies that connect the world with light become visible and the vast sea of those unknowing, seem like marionettes, jerked around by their restless minds.

Enchantment is the subtlest of magics that flaunts itself while remaining practically invisible and exudes great power while using no force whatsoever.

Elves Speak About "Home"

"To the elves, Paradise and Elfland and Home all mean the same thing." . . . . .

We elves strive to make ourselves at home everywhere.

If someone tells the elves to make ourselves at home, we do and start looking for closet space and dishes to do.

Among the Elfin, home and school are usually one.

Elves don't believe in homework for our children. However, since we often homeschool you could say that all their education is homework, although to them it would seem to be play.

You can often find the elves swaying or dancing to music only they can hear. It is the far distant sounds of Faerie reminding us of home.

Faeries, Pixies, Brownies, and Gnomes all are welcome in an elven home.

The difference between the elvish and most other folks is our homes are filled with singing, dancing, love, and laughter and theirs are often subject to the intermitten din of yelling, fighting, complaining, and mutual recrimination. It's that simple.
—observations by the elves

It is not that there are no monsters in Faerie—there are, near the edge where our worlds intersect with Man's. They are born of his fears and paranoia, his greed, jealousy and unwillingness to examine his own shadow. The deeper one goes into Faerie, however, the more wondrous everything becomes.

The road to Elfin always leads us home.

It is a curious thing about elves that they make thems'elves at home wherever they are and yet ever seem to be from a distant land.

"THERE IS SOMETHING ABOUT MIST THAT EVER REMINDS ELVES OF OUR HOME.". . . . .

In Elfland, nearly every home is a studio displaying arts, crafts or bartering food, and the streets are filled with buskers.

When things go really wrong, we elfin do the dishes and sweep the floors and in that way begin to set the world in order.

Most elves look upon housecleaning in the same way we view modern medicine, as something that you only do in an emergency.

The Oceans remind the elves of our home in Faerie.
The Forests remind us of our home as well, as do the Mountains.
The cities of Man, however, remind us that humanity is at least a bit insane and to be therefore cautions around them.

Elvenhome is not merely a place of beauty but place filled by an atmosphere of love.

If you ask the Fae what our favorite architectural buildings of man are, we most often answer, "Ancient Ruins."

Elves believe the best way to clean house is to move.

Some folks make little houses for the faeries. We make our whole house a sanctuary for elfin kind.

The homes of elves can best be described as any place the elfin live happily together.

The elves say home is not where you live but where your family abides.

What The Elven Say About Themselves

"SOME FOLKS INSIST THAT WE CANNOT BE ELVES BECAUSE WE ARE MORE THAN A FOOT TALL. WE SIMPLY SMILE AT THEM AND SAY, 'WE'VE GROWN'." . . . . .

One doesn't become an elf simply because they've blundered into Faerie. But wherever we elves go, Elfin swirls around us… like the Mist coming from the sea.

Being an elf isn't a matter of belief, it's a result of Being. We could be a leaf all day long but we'll eventually fall from the tree, but if we are the tree itself, we'll live eternally through the flowering of the seeds.

For the Faeries, glitter is not just an art supply, it's a way of life.

If you ask the elves what their favorite color is, they may very well tell you it is rainbow.

We elfin often have cause to pass through the world of the normal folk, but for us it is like someone swimming beneath the sea. We can swim beneath the ocean and explore the world of the fishes but we are ever aware that it is not our natural environment and we are only ever visitors there.

The elves often like to play curious mind games. They love to be courteous and kind to those who are less than so and to watch while such people either relax and are soothed on their way or leave screaming and tearing their hair out in frustration.

Surely one of the most observable of elfin traits is curiosity.

If you ask the elves what they seek,
They will nearly always say:
"To understand."

Elves are almost never influenced by peer pressure.
While we are peers with everyone,
We have no peers.

"DESPITE WHAT STORIES SAY, ELVES DON'T TEND TO LIVE IN KINGDOMS OR QUEENDOMS BUT IN FREEDOMS." . . . . .

We elves find the concept of normality an anathema to us . We are not normal in any sense of the word. Thus when people tell us that arguments and conflict are normal in relationships, we can but agree with them.

Some people think that we elfin are re-emerging in the world in order to take control. We find this idea laughable. We have not come to control the world but to set it free.

It is often written that we elfin have no souls. This is the most incredible gibberish. Not only do we have souls but also we are most often what people refer to as "old souls." Perhaps this is what confuses them. For we are so ancient that our souls have attained a degree of tranquility and quietude that it is as if it were not there at all.

The Elves love "found" things which they consider particularly magical.

We have often been called the "Good Neighbours" and that is certainly true. We not only look out for our own interests but our neighbours as well and anyone lucky enough to have the elfin as neighbours are lucky indeed.

Most elves do not practice rituals of marriage nor concern ours'elves with the legalities there of, except at times to "humor" the societies we find ours'elves by fate residing within. To us people either wish to be together or not and either way, should follow their hearts promptings.

We elves don't really believe in "eating and running" however, we have been often found to eat and glide off gracefully.

Elves feel no need to prove thems'elves, yet they do so with every breath.

Elves are like the ocean. We ebb and we flow. We advance and retreat. Yet we are ceaseless.

The elves say: "People sometimes tend to idealize us,
But we are more real than they imagine."

It is not easy to make elves laugh, yet they find most of life amusing.

"WHEN PEOPLE ASK US IF WE THINK ELVES REALLY EXIST, WE OFTEN PINCH OURS'ELVES AND SAY, 'WE SEEM TO EXIST.' PERHAPS WE SHOULD PINCH THEM." . . . . .

People sometimes ask us if we believe in elves, by which we assume they mean do we believe in ours'elves, and, of course, we do. We are very self-confident people.

In most cultures, artists are a small and segregated community within the society. However, among the elven, everyone is considered an artist and each member of elven society, no matter what they do, is encouraged to develop the creative aspect of their nature as well as do everything they undertake with grace, elegance and to the optimum of their ability.

We have been accused at times of thinking in "us and them" terms. We deny this. We elfin are eager to be friends with everyone. It is those who refuse to reciprocate that friendship that have defined thems'elves as "them."

We elfin cannot claim to have created lace, since we got the idea from the Spider people. But we have certainly done our best to elaborate upon it.

Some people are concerned that many of the individuals who claim to be elves are just wanabes. But that doesn't concern these elves at all, for we also want them to be elves or whatever it is they truly wish to be.

Elves being often smarter and more magical than most folks around us have been noted for a certain tendency toward arrogance. This is our karma. To master it we must learn patience and compassion.

When elves go traveling together they often say they are "on the wing."

We elves have been told that men say that if they stop believing in us, we will cease to exist. We shake our heads in wonder that men believe the most incredible things.

Nothing is more important to elves than love, Loyalty, Friendship, Honor, Family, Creativity, etc., etc.

Elves are prone to say, "Others may not believe in us, but we believe in ourselves."

"SOME FOLKS WRITE ABOUT 'TRUE BLOOD' ELVES, BUT WE ELFIN FIND SUCH IDEAS HUMOROUS. TO TRULY UNDERSTAND THE ELFIN, ONE NEEDS MUST CEASE TO THINK IN MATERIAL PARADIGMS. IT IS NOT TRUE BLOOD THAT MAKES US ELFIN, NOR POINTED EARS OR ANY SUCH AT ALL, BUT SPIRIT AND VISION AND THE LIVING BREATH OF ELFIN THAT ILLUMINATES OUR SOUL." . . . . .

Are we crazy for thinking we are elves? Perhaps, but that doesn't mean we are not elves.

We admit that we may not be elfin in the way that some people define elves but we are assuredly elfin in the way we elfin choose to define ourselves.

We don't mean to be conceited but we elfin are after all some of the most fascinating, elegant and adorable creatures ever created. Of course, we don't mean that about ours'elves individually but our others collectively.

Some folks when we reveal that we are elves clearly wonder what our problem is. But for we elves, being elfin is not the problem but the solution.

Decision-making among the elves is often a curious thing. They consider every angle of a problem until it seems they will make no decision at all. Yet when they do decide it is like an avalanche on a high mountain. Nothing can stop it once it begins.

In many ways life among the elven is much akin to a large family or an old country school. The older children are always taking care of the littler ones.

No one loves elves the way elves do, it is true. We are our biggest fans. Still, we are quite humble and dispassionate in our appraisal of ours'elves.

Only those of elfin spirit can see that our ears are pointed.

Some folks say we fae folk kidnap children. These elves have surely never done so. However, we have found that those children of all ages whose own parents didn't seem to want them, find acceptance among us and just don't want to leave. We nurture children of all ages.

"WHEN WE ELVES ARE TOLD TO STOP DOING SOMETHING THAT WE HAVEN'T DONE, WE OFTEN INTERPRET THAT TO MEAN WE SHOULD START." . . . . .

When elves are about to begin something totally new we often say we are "free falling."

You may think us cruel but when someone is rude to the elves we respond with courtesy and love which so baffles them that they are tortured endlessly, much to our delight.

We elfin tend to laud self-sacrifice much less than some folk but practice it more.

Honesty is a cherished virtue among we elfin, we only lie when we absolutely have to.

People often wonder how we elfin can still dance and sing when things are difficult and stressfilled. And surely it is not that we don't see and feel the suffering of the world. It is just that we don't wish to participate in it.

The elves are a bit like comets traveling through the realms and shedding light wherever they go.

If you wish to find the elves in any society, you need look little further than the artists, the dreamers, and the explorers.

The elves ever hope for the best, plan for the worst, and act toward the possible.

Do elves make claim to every thing good in the world? Yes, but we're always eager to share.

We elves seek to be familiar with the all of Nature.

Elves sometimes compare ours'elves to ripe cherries. Shiny on the outside, sweet on the inside, hard in the core. Yet it is that hard seed that gives birth to Evermore.

Elves are as independent as cats, as loyal as dogs, and as fierce as a mother defending her children.

"WHAT TRULY DEFINES THE ELVES IS OUR UNIQUE AND INDIVIDUAL BEINGS. THERE IS AN EXCEPTION TO EVERY RULE AND THE ELVES ARE USUALLY IT.". . . . .

What are elves like when they are alone? Thems'elves.
What are elves like when they are together? Thems'elves.

We elves often wonder why so many writers portray us as callous, cruel and capricious. But we suspect that they don't know how to make intelligence and kindness seem exciting. Yet to the elves, intelligence and kindness are the sexiest things of all.

Some tales say that one should never thank the fae. We elves find this a curious idea since we are quite big on courtesy. It is true that one should be sincere in thanking us, but even then if an insincere "Thanks" ultimately leads one to learn better manners, we are all for it.

Many think we fae to be capricious, but seldom is this so. There is intent to all we do, as the wise do know.

Trying to understand elves
Is like trying to understand a wild, creative genius.
It is far better to either help them or get out of their way.

Elves are the most logical of beings, which is why they nearly always trust their intuition.

Some folks claim that with the fae nothing is ever free,
That one must barter for everything,
As though we were common merchants.
The truth is, with us nearly everything is free.
We just appreciate reciprocation.

Arguing with elves is a waste of your breath and our time.

You would be better off trying to convert your cat than persuade an elf of the rightness of your religious beliefs.

"MOST PEOPLE ARE AFRAID AND AVOID THE HOMELESS AND THE STREET PEOPLE AND LOOK DOWN ON THEM. BUT WE ELVES KNOW THEM TO BE OUR VERY OWN FAERIE FOLK JUST SO DAMAGED BY THE WORLD THAT THEY CANNOT FIND AN EASY PLACE WITHIN IT."....

Some people say that the elves are wise, but the elves merely claim to be lovers of truth, beauty and all that is wondrous and magical in the world.

Elves nearly always recognize other fae when we encounter them. But normal folk merely see us as something strange that they only wish to see from the corners of their eyes.

If we elves were to compare ourselves to a food, it would probably be dark chocolate, though some might say pizza, or coffee or Masala Chai, or perhaps a rich smorgasbord of culinary delights.

The only thing you can really be sure of when dealing with elves is that you never know what they'll do next.

Elvish cuisine is very simple as it consists of good food and great food. Which is most likely why men are told never to eat or drink in Faerie lest they will become enchanted and unable to leave.

There is no aspect of life large nor miniscule which some elf doesn't find fascinating and is deep in research about.

When the sun comes out, the elves celebrate.
On a rainy day, we rejoice.
When it is overcast, we luxuriate in its quiet potentiality.
Are you beginning to get the idea?

Elves have almost no interest in arguing but have a great hunger to understand.

We elves may hide sometimes, but only because it is wise to do so, we are proud to be elfin.

Faerie calls to her own kind. If you hear the Call of Faerie, it is surely because you have, at least in part, some faerie blood. That is the nature of reality.

"MOST RACES SEEM TO REDUCE THEIR POPULATION THROUGH WAR AND DISEASE; THE ELFIN PREFER BIRTH CONTROL." . . . . .

To normal folk, nearly all elves seem eccentric. But to the elves, eccentricity is the norm.

If you ask the elves where they are from, they are likely to say "here and there."

Some people speak of half elves or of being part elfin, but we elven do not see it that way. To us, if you are half elven, you are elfin. If you are part elven, you are elfin. If you are a friend to the elves, you are elfin, too. If you wish to be elfin, you are as elfin as you wish to be.

The difference between the elves and most people is that they tend to take themselves seriously and we don't.

There's a difference between being selfish and being elfish. Selfish is all about "me." Elfish is all about "we."

In so much as there are elves who exist in human bodies and we can interbreed with man, we can be considered part of humanity, although we prefer to call it "hu-elvity."

Elves are such a diverse people that about the only thing you can say that applies to all of us is that we are magic.

Elves are a clever folk and they appreciate the clever, but they appreciate loving kindness more.

Elves are more inclined to encourage than criticize.

Elves ever remember those they love.

Faerie folk come in many shapes and forms. Not all of them are human. In fact, we are the very few.

Elves frequently make good therapists because one of our greatest powers tends to be the ability to understand.

The Silver Elves. . . .   69

Elven Sayings About the Apolcalypse and Other Such Nonsense

"SOME FOLKS TELL US THAT THE END IS RIGHT AROUND THE CORNER — WHICH IS WHY WE ELVES LIKE TO LIVE IN FORESTS WHERE THERE ARE NO CORNERS." . . . . .

Some people think the Apocalypse is ineveitable. We elves think it is the ineveitable consequence of obstinent stupidity.

Many people are waiting for the Apolcalypse. The Shining Ones are striving to avoid it.

"Point your ears in the right direction." An Olde Elven Saying meaning: Listen to the wise and ignore rantings of the foolish.

From the point of view of the elves it seems that man would rather believe and work toward an even impending apocalypse than believe in elves and Elfin.

The normal world reflects a black magic spell designed to convince us that we are not Faerie Folk and that, in fact, Faerie does not exist. Once you see through the spell, a world of wonder unfolds before you.

It is hard to believe that man would be so foolish as to destroy the world and himself but unfortunately it's true. Nonetheless, we remain optimistic. For we have seen the night sky filled with stars and know the truth beyond seeming.

The elves have observed that the world seems to go mad at times, but then tradition has it that those who are mad are more likely to see Faerie.

We elves sometimes call the Apocalypse the "End of an Error."

What the Elven Say About the World of Humans

ॐ

"THROUGH THE FOREST SLIP SILENTLY; AMONG MEN, DO THE SAME." . . . . .

The elfin are perplexed by the fact that the closer normal people live together, the further apart they get.

Many folk accuse us of not taking things very seriously. It's just as well, for if we did we would recommmend that most of the world's population be commited, for they are seriously insane.

Few people take the elfin very seriously, which is just as well for when they do so they tend to terrify thems'elves unnecessarily

There was a time when men first came and razed our forest for their farms that they would leave us milk and biscuits and other offerings outside their doors at night to placate us and offer tribute. Now they offer the elfin food stamps which is neither as personal nor poetic, but at least the milk is fresh.

Elves speaking about Mankind:
"We have watched helpless as they have murdered the trees, polluted the oceans and the atmosphere and have even treated the elves with callous disregard. They tell us it is not personal, simply business. However the fact they've done all this without feeling or animosity, somehow fails to comfort us."

We've often been told that war, conflict, rape, murder, and robbery are an inevitable part of life. And we elves must agree in so much as, as long as people believe they are inevitable, they will be.

Elves find Man's tendency to yell about nearly everything rather baffling.

The elves observing the world of men have concluded that Politics is a game in which all the players are expected to cheat.

Men seem to think that because their lives seem so short to them that they must be very special to the universe. We elves find that a curious logic.

"THERE ARE SOME PEOPLE WHO ARE SO DETERMINED TO CONVINCE WE ELFIN THAT THEY ARE RIGHT THAT THEY HAVE NOT NOTICED, WE HAVE LEFT." . . . . .

It is the most hopeless thing to try and conform and cater to the whims of the normals, since they don't even know what they really want.

Men and others often hunt animals and kill them for "sport." We elfin think that a very peculiar hobby.

Often when we encounter people, they return our smiles with looks of suspicion. We cannot but help feel the most incredible compassion for these folks.

Mankind tells us that they are the "Crown of Creation," which makes us wonder why they so often act like heels.

We elves are rather fond of the modern goths, which we cannot say concerning the medieval ones.

We elves do not aspire to change the world so much as we aspire to change ours'elves and in so doing transform all things connected to us.

There are certain folks who are always fighting and arguing with each other, each side certain that it is right. We suspect in time that they may kill each other off and it will be we elven who are left.

Some think we elves are too gentle for this sometimes violent world. But we see it as a wild horse needing to be tamed.

In a world where every man is for himself, the elves are for each other and everyone else.

Elves find it amazing that men think their Gods wish them to be obsequious sycophants. If we elves had Gods, we are certain they'd find such behavior as disgusting as we do.

There is at least one thing we elfin have in common to men. They seem to adore sports where balls are involved. We elfin also love to ball.

"WHEN MEN TELL US THEY KILL TWO BIRDS WITH ONE STONE, WE ELVES ALWAYS WONDER WHY ARE THEY KILLING BIRDS?". . . . .

The world is a potluck of magic. Be sure to bring your own.

The elves observe that for Man the hardest magic to make work is that of relationships.

If you are looking for certainty, ask man.
If you wish to know all the possibilities, speak to the elves.

Elves are appalled by mankind's unceasing war of annihilation with the viruses. We feel certain that if we could just get them to communicate with each other, they could work things out between them.

Perhaps you can understand our perplexity. Men cut down the trees to build houses that are hot in the summer and cold in the winter. Thus, he installs devices to cool and heat the place that takes electricity; so, he dams the rivers. And all of this cost lots of money, so he works most of the time and barely spends any time at home except to sleep. While he could have lived beneath the trees and been sheltered for nearly free. Does any of this make any sense to you?

Some people believe we dislike mankind and some other races. But this is not true. If anything, we are disappointed that they do not reciprocate the love and admiration we would so willingly render unto them.

When we elfin walk in the food stores of man, we find aisles of bloody and cut up carcasses of animals wrapped in cellophane. And men think that we are strange.

We have always felt different from them. Even when we tried to ignore that difference and make our place among them, they have always known we were different and treated us as such. Because they do not believe in elves, they do not believe us to be elven; but, we have come to understand that this is the nature of our difference and in accepting our elfin nature we have, at last, embraced our own.

Men are always telling us how 'tough' they are. A fact we find somewhat disconcerting since we've never even considered eating them. Don't they know we're vegetarians?

Elven Knowledge About the Wicked and Evil, Greed and Hate, War and Conflict

"ALL WARS AND CONFLICTS ARE ULTIMATELY BUT THE INEPT FUMBLINGS OF INEXPERIENCED LOVERS STRUGGLING TO FIND THEIR WAY INTO EACH OTHER'S ARMS." . . . .

Those who do wrong intentionally are wicked, those who do it accidentally are foolish. Folly can learn although it doesn't always realize it needs to do so. The wicked can change but it seldom desires to do so.

The enemies of the elves are always doing things to make us hate them. For hate is a disease of the soul and if they succeed in making us hate them they stand victorious. Thus, we always strive to go on with our lives happy and gleeful or sometimes peacefully resigned, as though our enemies did not exist, for this is our victory.

One can never understand someone they hate. A sympathetic compassion is the only tool for true insight into another being.

Kindness is more painful to the wicked than cruelty.

We'd love to say that we elfin are completely free of prejudice and hate but sometimes the most we can say is simply, "We're sorry."

"The elves say that until one reaches the light at the end of the tunnel, one must carry their own light amidst the darkened world." —Elven Knowledge

We are somewhat unclear as to why men and orcs and some others like to celebrate holidays by shooting off guns. Perhaps they think they are scaring away demons. We must inform them, however, that demons like guns.

"Even a small light becomes great when cast against darkness." Olde Elven Saying

If we are not in harmony with Nature then we are, de facto, at war with it and it is a war we can never win because to defeat the enemy is to destroy ourselves.

"SOMETHING MAGIC THIS WAY COMES, WICKED'S HAD ITS WAY TOO LONG." (ELVEN SONG VERSE) . . . . .

When asked to comment on the means to end war, the Great Elfin Sage Milovyn replied, "Make friends, create abundance and share love!"

Evil Magic is ultimately an oxymoron, for evil destroys the ecstasy that all true magic depends upon.

We've often heard men say that hate keeps them going. But we wonder, where is it that they are going to?

Many folks feel greed is what motivates them. The elves know it is what enslaves them.

Elves understand that everything is possible but some things are not meant to be. Evil is one of these.

"The Elves say the good must be strong and the strong must be good or evil will result." —Ancient Elven Knowledge

Those who look down upon we elfin and our humble ways might do well to reflect that we were conscious radiant beings of light in the universe when they were still protozoan living off the ooze and slime of the primordial morass.

We elfin, by nature, are a very lucky folk, and those who act against us thus draw down misfortune upon themselves without the elves even lifting a finger, for to interfere with luck is, by its very nature, ill omened.

The Elven say: The greedy always end by eating themselves.

It is the nature of evil to see the wicked in all things. It is the nature of good to see the light in all things. It is the nature of the elves to see both.

What the Elves Say They Believe and Don't Believe

"WE'VE HEARD THAT MAN BELIEVES HE WAS CREATED FROM MUD AND WOMAN FROM THE RIB OF THE FIRST MAN. WE ELVEN BELIEVE WE WERE SHAPED FROM STARDUST." . . . . .

The elfin do not believe in the superiority of the male over the female or the female over the male but believe in the power of a united people to master any quirk of fate and of the ability of a single elf bringing a greater light to all of us.

Elves believe administrators to be highly paid secretaries.

We've heard certain people say the Gods exist because they believe in them and die when they do not. By that same logic we expect they think that we elves don't exist because they don't believe in us. But we believe in ourselves and the Gods exist whether they believe in them or not as well. All they are doing with their belief is providing robes for the Gods to clothe themselves in.

Elves have an unshakable belief in the inevitable consequence of their infectious personalities... which is joy.

If you ask the elfin what we believe in, we'll most often reply, "Everything."

The elvish believe the best way to tame a demon is to cease to feed it.

Elves believe that Magic exists in potential in all things, only awaiting their intent to give it purpose.

The Elven say:
"It is easier to be something than believe you are something; therefore, do and be and allow belief to come in its own time."

When the Elves say the Universe is One, they do not mean it is the same but that it is all connected.

"WE ELVES BELIEVE THAT THE CROW'S CALL SUMMONS US TO GATHER." . . .
. .

The elfin frequently bend over backwards to help others in need. We believe stretching to be therapeutic.

We elfin often call the Aurora Borealis the dragon's breath. We believe the lights represent the descent to Earth of Angelic beings bringing gifts of power and enlightenment. We consider those who witness this phenomenon to be particularly blessed.

There is no Elfin religion, and we elves don't really believe in Gods and Goddesses quite in the way that most folks do. But if they did exist, we'd be having sex with them.

It's not really a matter of belief or an issue of faith, so much as a need to trust; and in doing so Elfin will come in its own time as a lover inevitably comes to their soul mate.

We elfin do not believe we are better than other people, we simply believe there are some folks who could do quite a bit more to live up to their full potential.

The elves believe every day has the potential to be the beginning of a great adventure.

We elves believe the Universe speaks to us and we may find its messages anywhere, thus we are ever listening.

Most folks want to believe in something bigger and greater than themselves. We elves simply wish to know the truth.

The Elves believe all the Universe is dancing.

What Say the Elven Magicans

"WITH THE RIGHT MAGIC, EVERY CHILL WIND CAN BE TRANSFORMED INTO A COOL BREEZE". . . . .

Most people think of magic as a power or tool that is directed by will or intent. And we do not deny there is truth in this. But we elfin see magic more as a relationship between ours'elves and nature and the universe, and when we are in the proper relationship with these elementals, the magic just happens.

Courtesy is an elfin magic that few understand but almost none can resist.

The power of magic is a gift from on high.

There are never any strings attached with Elfin.
It is ever a matter of free will.
It is only when the choice is free that magic is truly binding.

Someone could ask, and justly, if we are such powerful magicians, why has our Elven Culture nearly disappeared from this world? We can only reply, our magic is far from finished.

If you wish to learn magic, unleash your soul.

The Magic always resents being forced but responds well to persuasion and charm. Despite what some have written, we elves are not irrational beings. Nor are we out of touch with reality. We are simply in touch with a different Reality.

When your life is over, Your Magic is set free,
And then all that you have wrought, Comes to be.

The bible says, "In the beginning was the Word."
The elves say, "In the beginning was the Spell."

Elven magic is not so much about force as it is finesse.

"THE ELFIN SAY PUSHING THE MAGIC IS NOT NEARLY AS EFFECTIVE AS STROKING IT.". . . . .

We are told that eventually nearly all magicians must choose between the left hand path or the right hand path, however, we elfin nearly always choose the two handed path.

It is said that time flows differently in Faerie. That for those who come from the world and spend some time there, that years pass as though they were weeks. Which simply goes to prove the old adage that time flies when you're having fun.

Elves almost never try to dominate other people or situations in order to manipulate things to get our way. It is not that we don't believe in the power of the will but rather that we have learned that will power is most effective when applied to ours'elves.

Most people have a dichotomous view of the world in which something either is real or it is not. But we elves have a paradoxical view of the world in which things can be real and unreal at the same time. It is this philosophy that allows us to move through the world that normal folk consider real and still live within the Reality of Faerie, which intersects and overlaps it and function effectively in both.

Elfin magic is not about dominating others but mastering our own s'elves. In so doing our others yield to us willingly.

Magic is not about getting what you want by depriving others. True magic is about everyone getting what they need.

We elfin tend to approach the greater Spirits differently than most magicians. We do not attempt to compel the spirits to obey by the power of our will, as many traditional magi do. Nor do we, as the religionists, pray and bargain and supplicate with sacrifices. Rather, it is our way to charm the spirits with our elfin ways and thus enchanted they willingly bestow vast luck upon us.

The magical philosophy of the elves: Manipulation limits magic.

Elves are contagious. We turn everything we touch into elven magic.

For the elven, magic is as natural as drawing breath.

The Silver Elves. . . .   79

"IN ELFIN MAGIC, LIKE NEARLY ALL OF THE ARS MAGICA, THERE COMES A MOMENT WHEN YOU GIVE UP DOUBT AND SIMPLY DO. AND IN DOING, SUCCEED. AND IN SUCCESS, OVERCOME THE DOUBT WHICH PREVENTED YOU FROM DOING." . . . . .

In stories and in life, power is often shared in some object, like a ring or signet of a king, or an amulet or some symbol of office and authority. Such powers, however, always reside within the "office" itself and belongs to the individual only so long as they have the "ring" or symbol of authority in their possession. We elves seek not such power but instead to develop the powers that live in potential within our own being so that whether we are king or janitor, we will accomplish that office with the full power of a vibrant personality and soul.

We elves don't do magic to gain power nor even use it, but for the pure wonder of it.

Some say patience is a virtue. Elves call it a magic.

We elves are Alchemists. We mix love with happiness and smiles, and create magic.

The Elves like to say: "The world is an illusion. But as magicians it is our calling to make it the greatest illusion ever."

Every elf has a dragon within. It is our connection to the Divine Magic, the Magic of Creation.

"Every people have their wizards." Old Elven Saying meaning don't let prejudice blind you to talent and appreciate the genius in everyone.

Some folks speak of midnight as the Witching Hour. We elves speak of the Enchanting Time, which is when our beloved kindred arrive

Some people think there are two kinds of people in the world, those who choose realism and those who choose magic. But we elves are the third kind that chooses magic realism. We choose to make magic real.

Some folks think they can bottle up Elfin magic and keep it all to themselves but they are wrong. Elfin magic by its very nature ever seeks to be shared.

"ELFIN MAGIC IS NOT A PROCESS OF COMPELLING UNWILLING DEMONS TO DO OUR WILL, BUT ONE OF ENCHANTING BENEFICENT SPIRITS TO AIDE US.". . . . .

Most people think Magic is about telling the Universe what to do. Elves see magic as enchanting the Universe to fall in love with us so it does most of what we want without even needing to be asked.

When elves do martial arts, we often do Judo, Jujitsu, Akido, Capoeira, Kung Fu, and other flowing forms. Some might ask if elves have magic then why would they bother with martial arts, but elves will tell you martial arts are magic. But then to the elves, nearly everything is magic. Or if it is not, they will make it so.

They say love makes the world go around. Thus the elves use love to create magic and magic to create love and in this way keep the great dance spinning.

The Elven believe there is no effort no matter how small or subtle that does not find response in the Magic.

We Elfin say: "The beginning of the Magic is beyond time, but its fulfillment is within it."

Often the most difficult part of the Magic is waiting for it to fulfill itself. Other times, it is having the faith that it will do so. Ultimately, our faith in the magic is our faith in ours'elves. Which of us has never doubted themselves? And would you trust such a person?

To the elven, magic is not so much a craft to be learned and practiced or an occult power to be developed and used, as the basic underlying nature of life; and the more one becomes in tune with their own nature, the more magical, thus elfin, our life becomes.

The essence of Elfin Magic is to discover our true s'elves and in doing that all of Nature acquiesces to our will.

The ancient Elven Magic is not contained in lost tomes but secreted in the hearts and souls of the elves.

"SCIENCE IS THE METHOD; KNOWLEDGE IS THE KEY; LOVE IS THE PATH; AND MAGIC IS THE RESULT.". . . . .

Unlike most magical and esoteric groups, the elves do not make a great deal about the secrets to which they are privy. Whatever secrets they have are open secrets and available to anyone capable of understanding them. If someone asks the elves if they have secrets, they will reply, "None to speak of."

The Elves Say: "We make Faerie real as we live it. We make Magic real as we do it. We make love real as we share it. Love is Magic, Magic is Faerie, Faerie is Love."

When you're afraid, When you are worried, When you are obsessed, Transform those energies into magic. Empower your intent And watch the world realign.

The elves say: "The world is made of energy. Energy is light, and light is magic. Thus we live in a magical world."

Elven magic is both different and the same as other magics.
It is the same in that it is magic
And all magic comes from the same source.
It is different in that it is Elven.
Need we say more?

The Greatest Magic we can perform is being ours'elves.

Denying the existence of magic is like wearing dark patches over your eyes. You won't see much but it isn't because it's not there.

Every elf receives an inheritance from Faerie, it's called magic.

To traditional magicians, spirits are either demons to be compelled or powers to be implored; but to we elven the spirits are our friends, colleagues and kin, who are not only inclined to help us, but also easily persuaded to do so.

Those who use magic to engage in conflict do not understand the true nature of magic.

The goal of elfin magic is not to control people but to set them free.

Elves Speak About Stars and Starlight

"REMEMBER: IT IS IN DARKNESS THAT THE STARLIGHT IS REVEALED". . . .

.

As twilight ascends, we gather close, our desire keeping rhythm to the drum beats of our hearts, our elf eyes aglow with the expectation of what is in our minds already reality.

If we cast stardust on this page after we write this, will you see it? Do you?

The Stars are a map of our destiny.

If you look in an elfin heart, you'll find love; if you look in elvish eyes you'll see starlight.

When you wish upon a star the elves are listening.

Life is a journey, even when we sit in silent stillness the earth and the stars move us along.

"It is not enough to wish upon a star, one must also act upon their wish." —What Elven Mothers tell their Children

"We are born of starlight, made of starlight, destined for starlight." —Observation of the Elves

The Elfin believe they eat stardust and drink starlight which explains the radiant nature of their being.

Heaven is found through the pursuit of one's own star.

The stories of our people are varied yet they remain the same. We are many and we are one Here and among the Stars.

"The Earth speaks of fate and the Stars of Destiny." Olde Elven Saying.

"THE STARS COME DOWN TO TOUCH US, YET STILL STAY IN THE SKY." . . . .
—OLD ELVEN SAYING MEANING: ENLIGHTENMENT UPLIFTS THOSE WHO IT
TOUCHES WITHOUT LOSING ANYTHING.

The elves say a star is the home of billions of Shining Ones dancing together.

The Elves say that every star is the genius of the Magic unfolding.
We come from the stars. We return to the stars! We are made of star stuff. Do you understand now why elves often call thems'elves Star.

The more we become attuned to our true s'elves, the more we radiate the light of the stars within us.

Like the ancient mariners who use the stars to guide them across the seas, the elves use them to guide us through the lifetimes.

"If starlight is magic and all things are made of starlight, are all things magic? Yes, they are, say the elves. And on understanding that, you step closer to Faerie, which has been around you all along."
—Old Elven Knowledge

The goal of every elf is to awaken the starlight within.

Elves say: "We grant wishes and leave starlight in their eyes."

The woodland elves call stars the forest to be.

Elves refer to doing enchantment as weaving starlight.

When the Elven speak, the Stars pause to listen.

The elves believe that the Universe breathes starlight and we are that breath.

What Is Said About The Elven and Gift Giving

"ELVES ALWAYS BRING GIFTS. IT'S THEIR WAY OF PRIMING THE WELL." . . .
. .

One of the greatest gifts of the elves is our propensity for giving presents.

Elves can not be bribed for any price but are often charmed by gifts.

"We elves love presents, but the presence we love the most is yours."
—Elven Truth

The greatest gift you can offer anyone is the revelation of your true s'elf.

The elves love when the Angels visit for they always bring presents.

Elves share nearly everything among thems'elves, so much so that re-gifting might be considered a cultural philosophy.

There is a reason it's called The Present, for it is a gift beyond compare.

The principle of elven gifting is thus: when possible always reciprocate with a little bit more, this creates a cycle of giving that leads to great abundance shared by all.

Elves shower blessings and gifts upon our friends and ever wish to be friends with everyone and so those who insist on being our enemies are viewed as being especially ignorant.

We don't make offerings to the spirit world in order to obtain our desires. Our gifts are freely given because of our love of the spirits. If they for their part should return that love by granting our wishes, then we are truly thankful and consider ours'elves blest.

What Elves Say About the Journey to Elfin

"THERE ARE MANY PATHS TO ELFIN AND EVEN MORE WHEN YOU ARRIVE."
. . . . .

The deeper you wander into Elfin the greater your luck becomes!

The first step into Elfin begins with desire, the last ends with an embrace.

The Journey to Elfin is a trip all elves are on together although not always at the same time.

Contrary to what most folks think, Faerie is ever ready to embrace you. You just need to reach out.

The essence of Elfin is revealed at the end of every true faery tale. No matter what the challenges, obstacles, and dangers encountered on the way, in the end those who have been true to the principles of Faery always live "happily ever after."

When people first begin to see us, it is usually out of the corner of their eyes or under the influence of some intoxicant. But the deeper they move into Elfin, the more they realize that the people they've always dismissed as eccentric or weird and sometimes those they've passed by without noticing because they've seemed so very plain have all the time been in actuality the fair folk, disguised by society's determination to deny we could even exist.

The entrance to Elfin is as open as our heart and as closed as our mind.

Elves say: "If life were easy, we'd be living in Elfin."

Elven Saying: "We hear the voice of Elfin in the breeze stirring the leaves. We see it in the moonlight filtering through the mists. We smell it in the fertile damp of the deep woods. We taste it on your lips. But we feel it, always feel it, deep within."

The Passage into Faerie is always open, although the door you are trying may be closed.

If there were no such place as Elfin in the world it would still exist within our hearts.

"CURIOUS AS IT IS, OFTEN THE GREATEST BARRIER TO AN INDIVIDUAL ENTERING ELFIN IS THEIR REFUSAL TO LET GO OF THEIR SUFFERING.". . . .

The road to Elfin cannot be found on any map, nor is there a path that leads directly there. It's winding, twisting passage is found more often through serendipity and whimsy than unbending intent and will power.

A visit to Elfin is such a profound experience that while some forget they were ever there they are forever haunted by an indescribable longing to return.

"One cannot carry baggage to their grave nor enter Elfin with their clothes on." Old Elven Saying

Finding one's way into Elfin is no more difficult than being continually kind.

We are all returning to Elfin from different directions and the path that is right for you may be the wrong way for another.

If you ask the elves where they've been, they may very well say, "Here." If you ask them where they are going, they may also say "Here." To some this may seem evasive, but to the elves, it is a most evident and literal truth.

There are some who seem to think that if they could find the door to Elfin they would step inside and then suddenly their life would be better. It is our experience that as we make effort to improve ours'elves and our lives, Elfin gradually opens up to us.

Some people say the path to elfin is winding and crooked, but that is usually because many of those who tread it are confused and uncertain at first. Elves are great proponents of the path of least resistance and seek the easiest way to do nearly everything. Thus the road to Faerie is simple. One needs but be true to one's own fae nature and all else follows therefrom.

Most people spend their whole lives planning and preparing...but Elfin comes unawares.

The door into Faerie requires one to step over the line that separates the normal from the possible.

"THE SUREST WAY TO ELFIN IS THE UNCERTAIN PATH, THOSE WHO KNOW EXACTLY WHERE THEY ARE GOING SELDOM ARRIVE THERE.". . . . .

There are some who seem to think that if they could find the door to Elfin they would step inside and then suddenly their life would be better. It is our experience that as we make effort to improve ours'elves and our lives, Elfin gradually opens up to us.

The road to Elfin cannot be found on any map,
Nor is there a path that leads directly there.
It's winding, twisting passage is found more often
Through serendipity and whimsy
Than unbending intent and will power.

Elfin is not built with bricks and mortar, concrete or wood; it's not even built with trees and vines, but by the shared wishes and desires of the elven.

Elfin is a Fantasy born of Reality and a Reality created from Fantasy.

All roads lead to Elfin, but sometimes it is not the path you're on so much as the way you travel.

Every act of kindness, every effort to create beauty, every expression of love, leads us deeper into Elfin.

In Elfin, even the stones have a voice.

The more we become in touch with our own inner being, the deeper we are in Elfin.

Always as one comes to the heart of Elfin and strives to understand what the elves are all about, one comes to the notion of play.

If you want to find Elfin, look around you. If you wish to enter Elfin, look within.

The path to Elfin is found at the crossroads of imagination and possibility.

There is a flower we can eat that transports us to Elfin. It grows there.

"TO ENTER ELFIN ONE MUST ENTER THE REALM OF IMAGINATION, NOT AS A FANTASY, BUT AS A REALITY." . . . . .

The Path of the World tells one they must constantly conform to succeed. The Path to Elfin says that one can never succeed by being other than their true S'elf.

Always as one comes to the heart of Elfin and strives to understand what the elves are all about, one comes to the notion of play.

Elfin, like love and trust, cannot be stolen, coerced nor bought, although many are those who have tried. It can only be gifted, or sometimes won, by those with the courage to believe, the stamina to try and the faith to persevere when it seems all you are pursuing is an empty dream.

"The closer one comes to Elfin the more amazing the journey becomes." —Words of an Elfin Wyzard.

To the elves every dawn is a new dawn of Elfin.

The Light of Elfin is seen by the eye but recognized by the heart.

Fact about Elfin: "It is not simply that we long for Faerie but that Faerie longs for us as well."

Elfin is not so much a state on Earth or a territory thereof, as a state of mind, attitude and being. This, perhaps, explains why we elves tend to be less territorial than most folks.

When we harmonize with Nature, extending its wonder and beauty, we help create Faerie.

Your emotions are not your feelings, nor your thoughts your mind; when you realize this you step closer to Faerie than you've ever been.

The world can be a difficult place for the Elfin folk. We are going *Walk About* here and like all adventures it can be dangerous. But when we return to Faerie, which we inevitably will, we will be wiser, more knowledgeable and with a greater power to enchant.

"Elves value the advice of animals as much as that of humans,
sometimes more since animals don't tend to lie to us."

—Ancient Knowledge of the Elven Sorcerers

What Say the Wise Elven Sorcerers?

"IF YOU WISH TO KNOW THE TRUTH ABOUT SOMEONE, LISTEN CAREFULLY TO WHAT THEY SAY ABOUT YOU AND APPLY IT TO THEM." . . . . .

"When the fae get tortured in life, they can come out to be pretty odd ducks, but you just have to love them and then they bloom and brighten."—Silver Flame of the Silver Elves

True victory is not to be found in winning battles, nor winning a war, but in bringing an end to the need for conflict.

We elves deal not so much with the concrete mind as the verdant awareness.

The greatest power is that which arouses willing acquiescence.

Elfin is an intoxicating place, the water you drink, the food you eat, scent of flowers and the very air are like the most powerful psychedelics and aphrodisiacs and ecstasy producing substances one has ever encountered.

"The truth is revealed even in lies." — An Old Sorcerer's Saying

Every time an elf speaks, the elf casts a spell. Every time an elf listens, the elf creates an enchantment.

Every book is a threshold to another realm. Most, however, merely open the door to the rest room. And others, a broom closet so cluttered one labors to get through it. But a few are portals to a magical world so wondrous that one returns transformed.

No matter how great a wizard of fantasy may be, he is not greater than a real wizard no matter how humble his powers may be.

Always be your true s'elf, unless you're forced to pretend to be normal and then glamor those fools like crazy.

"Within is the way without." —Olde Elven Sorceres Saying meaning: it is by way of our feelings, minds and psyches that we may relate to the whole of the Nature.

Quotes about the Elfin Language
and Elven Names

"In truth, there is but one genuine Elfin language and that is the language of love. But of its dialects, there are as many as the stars." .....

There are words without meaning and there is meaning without words. That is what the Elfin language truly is, Love for which there are no words.

Elven Names are a magic that grows greater with use,
The more they are spoken the more Faerie's loosed,
To spread through the world and thus it to sway,
The hearts that do hunger for the bright Elven Way.

It is the opinion of the Elven that the power of a True Name is not nearly as potent as the power of True Love.

The Elfin language is not primarily a language of words but of tones.

One can utter elfish words and never be speaking Elven, yet one could speak any language in the Universe with a sincere heart and be speaking the secret language of the elves

"A name has no power without meaning." Elven Saying

We elves say it is not the name that makes the elf but the elf that makes the name.

An elf smile is a language of its own.

We elves name our swords because we believe all things have soul, spirit, power and personality.

The secret language of the Universe is Life. Those who understand this language read meaning everywhere. Alas, those who are unprepared for this are often viewed as insane.

"AN ELVEN NAME IS LIKE A PASSWORD THAT UNLOCKS A SECRET WORLD OF MAGIC AND MYSTERY." . . . . .

An elven name is a gift of magical power. Those who are not ready for that power, cast away their name and seldom, if ever, use it and often soon forget it.
—Ancient Elven Wisdom

Every time an elf name is spoken, it is like a bell rung into the world awakening the fae all around it.

Elves often accumulate names the way soldiers collect medals, athletes collect trophies, and Boy Scouts collect badges. In the end, we often have more names than the old Spanish Dons and more titles than the great Emporers. Still amoung ours'elves, we most often go by a simple nickname, sometimes just a single letter and the only titles that really matter to us are those of endearment.

We elves for the most part have normal names that we use to pass through the world of the normal folk. Some mistakenly refer to these as our real names, but they real-ly don't know what they're talking about.

A group of fish is called a shoal. A group of crows is called a murder. What do you call a group of elves? Why a party! The Next time you're in a restaurant and hear something like "Love: Party of Seven," look for the pointed ears.

It is said by some that everytime a bell rings, an angel gets his wings. We elves say everytime an elven name is spoken, enchantments burst into being.

The language of the elves is the language of the heart.

In the Elfin language the word play has a variety of connotations. It means play as most folks would use it, as in the children are at play or let's play a game. But it also carries the meaning of "practice" as in let's practice the violin. And it even bears the connotation that most folks would ascribe to the word work. So the elfin might say, "Let's go to play" and mean the same thing as most would mean saying, "Let's go to work." Only without the work part, of course.

Does one need an elven name to be an elf? Not at all. An elf is an elf no matter what we call ourselves. However, it is a bit of starlight that helps light the way to the deeper reaches of Faerie.

"THE FAERIE CLAIM THAT GLITTER IS A LANGUAGE AND PEOPLE WHO DON'T UNDERSTAND GLITTER ARE ILGLITTERATE." . . . . .

Elfin is not so much a language of love as a language of loving.

An elf name is the fae's personal mantra. One can chant it repetitively to focus one's awareness and increase one's personal power or the elf can chant another's name to empower that particular elf.

There is no such thing as bad language, just language used badly.

If you're given an elf name, cherish it. It contains more magic than most normal folks experience in a lifetime.

An elf name opens a door and allows magic into one's life.

Silver Speech, the language of The Silver Elves salutations (see our book titled *Arvyndase* for a complete guide to speaking and writing Silver Speech):
Kyela (Love)

Tae Arvyn Eldali (pronounced tay -- air - vin -- L - dah – lie, The Silver Elves)

Ver nesidas mellun vari te (In shimmering starlight ever be)

Eli Feln Le (We love you)

Fost Tae Lodver (Touch the truth)

Keldas Zet Ton Na Tarsalunin Sol (Running wild on a moonlit night)

Fardas Lovur Tae Lan (Dancing toward the dawn)

Ver tae Cysyldas dain ATA (In the Beginning was ONE)...

Fost nar Harno (Touch and Presence).

Usco tae melli alundir (beneath the stars radiant)

Elven Quotes About Dancing and Celebrations

஍

"If you look through the corridors of time, you'll find the elves dancing." . . . . .

Some elves talk, some elves listen. Some elves dance until we glisen.

"Sometimes you just have to dance." —Old Elven Saying

If you ask the elves what they celebrate, they will likely reply, "Nearly everything."

Elves don't march to a different drummer; we dance.

Elfin Magic, Elfin Light, shines beneath the full moon night.
Stars in heaven, fires aglow, we dance till dawn, true love to know.

Elves love holidays and celebrations. We love Halloween, Yule, birthdays and anniversaries. But our very favorite day to celebrate is called Today.

We elves do not have separate events for males and females. To us that would be as silly as having separate events for blonds and brunettes.

When the elves speak to their childern about the seasons being created by the wobbling tilt of the Earth, they explain that the Earth is dancing.

If you wish to know who has faerie blood all you have to do is turn on the music and see who starts tapping their feet, swaying to the music and dancing.

To the elves the Faerie Rade is like holy pilgrimage except instead of praying we are dancing and singing all the way. It is hoped that every elfae will go on one at least once in their life and preferably many times.

Many people think we elves spend all our time celebrating. And this is true if you realize that our celebrations are not entirely unlike the way a priest celebrates the Mass. Not that our celebrations involve ritual for they do not necessarily do so, but that our celebrations also revel in sacred, miraculous, and magical aspects of life.

"Fantasy stories often write of a hatred between elves and dwarves or elves and grimlins, goblins and orcs. And while it is true that we are less inclined by Nature to socialize with some of these folk and while some of them seem to have an instinctive dislike for us; we never judge anyone on the basis of their race. We have lived with dwarves and gnomes. We have been friends with and helped at times by grimlins, goblins and orcs. We judge each person by the virtue of their individual nature and actions. That is the Elven Way." —Old Elven Knowledge

What the Elves Know

"IT IS EASY TO TRIP OVER A ROCK WHEN YOU ARE WATCHING EVERYONE ELSE'S FOOTSTEPS." . . . . .

The greatest musical instrument is the heart.

There's an inner quiet to the elfin that many assume to be aloofness, it is instead the result of their experience in the transitoriness of all things and their belief in the Eternal Truth of the Temporal.

We elfin always approach life with a certain humility for we have discovered that it is a lesson life teaches whether one wishes to learn it or not.

There was once a time when we elfin had great powers in the world but that time is long gone and the world has passed, for good or ill, into other hands than our own. And yet, while we have but small powers in the world, we consider ours'elves to be some of the luckiest folk within it and not the least of that feeling comes from our never ending thanks to the great spirits for having given us the luck to be born elfin.

Decision-making among the elves is often a curious thing. They consider every angle of a problem until it seems they will make no decision at all. Yet when they do decide it is like an avalanche on a high mountain. Nothing can stop it once it begins.

"The truth is revealed in all things." —Ancient Elven Knowledge

The elves say: "Life changes everything."

Elfin Saying: "Magick is like a clear spring ever flowing."

Elves do not go on blind faith but faith based on our clear knowledge of the laws of Nature and the Universe.

Faerie is often called the realm of enchantment, which should tell one something about the true nature of the elves.

"IF YOU TRY TO UNDERSTAND THE ELVES, YOU ARE LIKELY TO WIND UP WITH THEM KNOWING EVERYTHING ABOUT YOU." . . . . .

What is an elf's duty? It is to become the best one can be and to help others do the same.

We are not elves because our parents were elves or our ancestors were elves but because we love all things elven.

Elves, like our cousins the vampires, are somewhat prone to ennui. However, then we rouse our spirits and remind ourselves that if we are looking for the world to be different than it is, it is we who must create that change.

"Life is by its nature symbiotic. We can only succeed together."
—The Wisdom of the Elves

Being an elf isn't a matter of belief, it's a result of Being.

We elves have heard that life is not a rehearsal and we elves agree and yet we ever seek to improve our performance knowing that the show goes ever on.

The elves say that when you solve a mystery you realize it was only a clue and the greater Mystery is dancing ever beyond, continually amazing and enticing us.

We elves put great store in the development of the personality, but only as a reflection of the soul.

Many elven are fascinated with Dragons. Even though they can be quite cantankerous concerning their great wealth, we find them often to be brilliant beings from whom we can learn many things.

If you ever doubt yours'elf and your magic, feed your unicorn.

If I were you ... I wouldn't be me and thus I would do whatever you'd do.
—Elven Philosophy about Giving Advice

The elves say that you can be whatever you wish, but you become whatever you do.

ELVEN SAYING: "HOW CAN WE COMPLAIN IF A DONKEY ACTS LIKE AN ASS?". . . . .

Describing Elves is like describing the shimmering hues of a rainbow.

It is only fair that we give them due credit. For we must admit that the gremlins and goblins seem to have a natural talent for bureaucracy

Occasionally people tell us that our elevator doesn't go to the top floor. That does not concern us because we feel certain that if need arises we will levitate to the top.

Some people call them ley lines — the paths of energy that crisscross the earth and here and there intersect, creating vortices of power. Others call them the hidden roads or the secret paths. And it is said, that the ancient Sidhe would go on Faerie Rades, traveling these secret byways and drawing luck down from the Moon and Stars and upward from the Earth, herself. There are those who try to map these lines and think themselves wise in their knowledge but we elfin know that it can't be done. The paths are ever changing. However, if you follow the path of spirit, facing life with courage and a bit of humor, the ways will be revealed to you. And you will never run out of luck.

One of the greatest challenges to the elfin soul is arrogance. We are aware of our position as "superior" beings but we must endlessly remind ours'elves that this is a circumstance of Fate, not an aspect of Destiny.

A unicorn without a horn is still a horse. —Olde Elven Saying meaning: Everyone has their own special magic and need only be their own true s'elf.

A unicorn with a horn is just a horse. Olde Elven Saying meaning: Beware of those who claim to be more than they really are.

The elves say that Life is the Neverending Story. It also has no beginning. It always was and ever will be. Both is and isn't at the same time. Is everywhere and nowhere simultaneously and is like a snake regurgitating its own tail.

The path to Elfin is illuminated by the light of those who have tread it before us.

"Elfin makes everyone beautiful." —An Old Elven Saying meaning exactly that.

"Don't rush the river."
—Ancient Elfin Admonition meaning: no need to be impatient about things that are only going to take their own time anyway.

Ancient Elfin Admonition

❧

"ONE CAN NEVER FREE THEMSELVES BY CONTRIBUTING TO THE OPPRESSION OF OTHERS".....

If you have nothing good to say... at least, say it politely.

We can hardly blame man and other races for following their own natures. It is their constant failure to do so that disappoints us.

"Don't expect the unexpected; prepare for it."
—An Admonition to elven warriors.

A spiteful tongue strangles it's owner from within.

There are no if, ands or buts in Magic, there is only Do or Not Do; and sometimes, when things go astray, Do-Do, which ultimately means we must Do it again.

In the long run, we either learn to be patient or we become a patient.

The motto of the Dominance Clique is "Divide and Conquer." The Seelie elf motto is, "United we shall overcome."

Be not like the wind that announces it's coming, but like the breeze barely noticed as it passes by.

If you attempt to pour your heart out through your mouth it tends to stick in the throat. Patience now, let it sing and every word will hum with magic.

Those who rewrite history in an attempt to fool others wind up deceiving themselves.

Faerie whispers an eternal message:
"Be Yours'elf, Be Magic, Help others do the same."
— An Admonition To Follow Into Faerie

Most people put up signs that say "No Trespassing,"
Elves erect signs that proclaim "This Way!"

— The Silver Elves

Elven Words to Remember

"If you think we're talking in circles, it's because you don't understand. When you do we'll proceed." . . . . .

The only thing more ignorant than a person who knows nothing is a person who knows everything.

A civilization can be judged by the amount of public restrooms they make available.

Everyone looks at the world from where they are standing at the moment.

We elves admit that we are often swayed by beauty... but always propelled by destiny.

Tomorrow never comes. The next life is just another day.

It takes two to tango but only one to start a fight.

Some folks mistake "similarity" for "sameness."
The elves are all similar in many ways, but none of us are the same.

The elven say that if you wish to understand others, one must remember that people do not hear their own voices as others hear them.

The elves say that the best way to honor the past is to create a better future.

Elves never tell people to "get lost," We just let them follow us deeper and deeper Into the Forest until they are found.

"Don't assume a Dragon will pick up the tab."
—An Old Elven Saying meaning: The wealthy are not always generous, thus one must ever be ready to pay one's own way.

"We'll find a way."
—Elven Saying

"ELVES THINK THAT OPINIONS ARE LIKE PENNIES. EVEN IF YOU PUT THEM ALL TOGETHER, THEY DON'T USUALLY AMOUNT TO MUCH." . . . . .

"You can't go to sea without getting wet." —Old Elven Saying, meaning: Every effect has its cause and every path its dangers.

There is a certain s'elf confidence that elves radiate that is so powerful that even when they answer "maybe" to a question—which is often— you feel they have told you something definite.

Elves frequently ask "why?" But they also ask "why not?"!

Every nomad has an oasis.

Worry is a box with no contents.
—Elven Saying

At some point, our inner radiance penetrates all the cells of our being and we are transformed.

Fate is the path that leads from our Karma to our Destiny.

"One may put out honey but can never know what bees may come to it." Olde Elven Saying to Remember.

The goal of the path is to travel.
The destination... the Way.
The road is never ending
The voices of destiny say.
—Gypsy Elf Song

Most people await some outer event,
Person or circumstance to make them happy.
The Elfin do not wait for happiness;
We create it. —Elven Creed We Live By

While others wish to rise above their peers and subjugate those below them, we elves' greatest wish is for others to join us in joy and celebrate.

The Elves Speak about Sex and Love Making

"CERTAIN RACES MAKE A BIG DEAL OUT OF SEPARATING SEX AND LOVE. WE ELVES MAKE A BIG DEAL ABOUT UNITING THEM." . . . . .

We elves are sometimes accused of having "sex on our minds." Although, we prefer to think of it as always having love in our hearts.

There is no such thing as prostitution among the elves. It is not that we are morally opposed to people selling sex. But why should anyone pay for what is, among us, nearly always freely available?

Men, perhaps because they believe they are mortal, think the primary purpose of sexual relations is procreation. Elves knowing our souls to be immortal believe the primary result of intercourse is creation. For there is almost nothing more inspiring to us then romance.

Old Elvish saying: "Love doesn't cease when the sex is over."

The romantic images of gypsies and pirates often appeal to the elven for romance ever springs from the soul of Faerie.

Among the elven, everyday is essentially Valentine's Day.

The Elves say: Love, Happiness and Laughter mixed together are the panacea of the Soul.

Elves neither lead nor follow but often we wander together in the same direction as we so enjoy each others company.

When we elves ponder upon how obsessed men are with sex, we realize we must be related after all.

"We elves are sometimes called the Rainbow folk
because we come in all colors."
—Wise Elven Saying

And Many More Silver Elves' Quotes
For the Modern Elf

"THE WORLD IS A CHAOTIC STORM. ELFIN IS ITS CALM CENTER." . . . . .

We elves love cosplay, although we don't tend to mimic characters so much as create our own. In that way we are rather like Tauriel who wasn't written about in the book but implied. Our characters are implied by the nature of Elfin.

Elves are like streams, we love to meander.

Elves are creatures of paradox. We are well aware that all things exist and don't exist simultaneously, which is confusing to most folks but makes perfect sense to us.

Olde Elven Saying: "The time is always now."

The great revelations in life come from personal contact with those who truly know and live their enchantments, not from books. Yet, we love books. They help show us the way, hint at possibilities and keep us company when we can't always be with our others.

Elves don't drink; we savor.

Elves view everything we do as works in progress.

"If you are looking for surprises, wander aimlessly."
—Elven Saying

Life is too long to concern ones'elf with unimportant things.

The true power of illusion is the wonder it arouses.

"Together Our Magic Is Stronger By Far!"
—Group Chanting Spell of the Silver Elves

The foolish assume they are wise.

"MODERN ELVES GENERALLY SEE OUR MISSION AS THE REIFICATION OF FAERIE." . . . . .

Elves look upon those who are racist, sexist or unreasonably prejudiced as being dimwitted.

Elves seldom fear what others may think.

"Let the rain come in its own time." Olde Elven Saying meaning: in as much as possible let Nature take its course and don't interfere unless you absolutely have to do so.

Elves view zealotry as a form of insanity.

Some folks try to argue with the elves, but elves for our own part usually just smile and continue on our chosen path.

Elves think more in terms of synthesis and synergy than in strict dichotomies.

The elves are involved in an ongoing conspiracy to make the world a better place using love, magic and beauty as their tools.

Elves don't laugh much, yet we have a great sense of humor. It would be true equally to say that nearly everything and almost nothing amuses us.

Some people accuse the elves of living in a fantasy world.
We do!
It's wonderful!
Why don't you come join us?

Being tricky isn't a habit of the pixies,
It's a hobby.

We elves believe the past still exists in the present, only transformed.

The Truth is: "Sometimes the answer is Chocolate."

"WE'RE NOT FANS OF THE LORD OF THE RINGS SO MUCH AS WE ARE IT'S LIVING EMBODIMENT IN THE MODERN WORLD." . . . . .

From the point of view of the elves, every person who strives to be the best version of hirs'elf sHe can be is doing magic.

We really shouldn't be surprised when we tell normal people we are elves and they don't believe us. After all, we've spent ages casting a glamor upon them to convince them we don't exist. Their disbelief is really just an affirmation of the power of our enchantments.

Elves consider fanaticism to be the sign of an inferior mind.

People sometimes tell us they don't believe we are elves. We smile and think: then why are they arguing with us?

You don't have to prove you're an elf to anyone. You just need to be your own elf.

Who has a greater right to define what elves are than we who are elves?

When young elves are told to *see like a Hawk*, it means they should examine things carefully from a far before becoming involved.

The world is merely the appearance of spiritual reality.

When the elves call someone a "bow without a string," they mean that the individual still needs to learn and develop something as a spirit in order to reach their full potential.

The Elves say: "Be kind to those who are less intelligent for if it wasn't for them we wouldn't seem so very smart."

Faerie may be an Illusion but it is much closer to the true nature of reality than that world that calls itself real.

When you open the way to Faerie, you are flinging wide the door to endless possibility.

"WORRY IS AN ATTEMPT TO UNRAVEL A KNOT BY PULLING IT TIGHTER."
—OLD ELVEN SAYING. . . . .

"Even dragons have scales." —Olde Elven Saying meaning that even the very powerful seek to protect themselves and therefore fear their vulnerabilities.

In the old days, Elf arrows were said by some to be poisoned darts shot from hiding. However, in modern times we elves think of them as potent ideas that penetrate the consciousness of the recalcitrant.

Being an elf is its own reward.

Magic is like a wild creature that one needs to tame without breaking.

When people ask us what we do, we elves often answer, "We understand."

"An arrow without a point seldom penetrates the target." Olde Elven Saying meaning: One needs to develop one's mind and logic to see to the heart of life.

The Elven philosophy is basically common sense combined with a very wide understanding of the nature of reality.

To the elves the Greenman is not a god but a brother.

The elves follow public opinion from the shadows of the forest, occasionally shooting elf darts at it.

It really shouldn't surprise us that corporations and other institutions should do such stupid things. After all, they are not really a person and they don't actually have a brain.

Most of those who are lost in the world have long ago given up wandering.

The decision to be your true s'elf is one of the most profound and important decisions of your life.

The ignorant think they know everything.

There are only two ways out of Life: Onward and Upward.

The way to an elf's heart is through your own.

Elf folk are catalysts. Wherever they go things begin to happen.

If you wish to bring the world into balance you must first balance yours'elf.

The Elves say: "We are One Mind with many points of view; One Heart with Singular Devotion to Faerie."

The Elves say: "There are rules and then there's reality."

Saving the world is rather like doing the dishes. You periodically have to do it over and over again.

Those who think they can use peer pressure to affect the behavior of elves don't understand the essential nature of the elfin.

Elves believe that a person without a sense of humor is deprived of one of their most important senses.

The proper study for the elves is Everything.

We elves don't have followers, we have come along for the ride'ers.

"The Way to the Past is through the Future." Olde Elven Saying.

"A nockless arrow cannot fly far." —Olde Elven Saying meaning: A good foundation in life is important for success.

Elves consider all people to be magical; it's just that most haven't realized it as yet.

"You can't go to sea without getting wet." —Old Elven Saying, meaning: Every effect has its cause and every path its dangers.

Grimlens often tell us there are two types of people in the world. Those who take what they want and those who get taken. Elves also believe there are two types of people in the world. Those who are simple minded enough to believe such bullshit and those intelligent enough to understand the world is a nuanced and myriad place.

We elves don't live beneath the earth so much as beneath the notice of the normal folk. They see us but never recognize us for whom we truly are.

Elves view fanaticism as a mental disorder unless it is a fantical love of all things Elven and Faerie and then, of course, it is perfectly understandable.

We elves often see ours'elves as re-distributers. We gather the magic we find about us each day and spread it to where it is needed, like bees spreading pollen.

If you were to use one word to summon up the elven philosophy, you may wish to use the word *rapport*.

"Magic loves surprizes." Old Elven Saying meaning: Magic manifests at the most unexpected times.

"Do your best in all you do and the best will always come to you." — Olde Elven Saying.

When children ask us how they can see faeries, we tell them that faeries often disguise themselves as dragonflies, butterflies, moths and fireflies. This is true, although it takes elven eyes to see it.

Everyone has two beasts in them. One is a dragon of immense power. The other is a Unicorn of great goodness. You must feed them equally lest great power should arise without goodness or goodness be rendered powerless.

The Elves have a saying: Be a Mother. Which means not only that one should be kind and nurturing to others, but one should make every day and everything one does, magic. For the elves note that everyone has a Mother and everyone a Father and yet observe that something so Universal and commonplace as parenthood can be so powerful and amazing that not only can they make each day special but they can influence one's entire life.

"THE SAD FACT OF MODERN LIFE IS THAT MOST FOLKS ARE SO CLUELESS THAT THEY DON'T EVEN REALIZE THAT LIFE IS A MYSTERY." . . . . .

Self Initiation is no more nor less valid than that given by a coven or organization. All true initiation evolves from genuine accomplishment and is granted by Life and followed by increased power and understanding. Ceremonies are merely the recognition of Initiation. They are not Initiation itself.

Life is a process of being and becoming at the same time. As we strive to be what we will become, we become ever closer to what we truly are. Be magic. Be Elfin.

For elves, magic is assumed to be the essential nature of Life.

To the elves, magic is as normal as having breakfast and as exciting as falling in love.

We elves don't entirely have a concept of being lost. To our minds, we are merely taking an unexpected detour.

The rules of elven archetecture are simple. Beside being structurally sound, every building is expected to be uniquely beautiful.

If you are going in the right direction, the signs will confirm it. If you go astray, the signs will guide you back.

There is a certain s'elf confidence that elves radiate that is so powerful that even when they answer "maybe" to a question—which is often— you feel they have told you something definite.

For elves enchantment is as effortless as breathing.

Faerie is as real as we make it.

Elves give little criticism and a lot of encouragement.

The Forest holds many secrets and they are all magical, but not all of them are kind.

If the elves tell you to Be Faerie, they are encouraging you to be fully yours'elf at your very best in the most enchanting and magical way possible.

"WAITING FOR THE RIGHT MOMENT IS ONE OF THE GREATEST OF MAGICAL POWERS." . . . . .

Faerie is so radiant that some folks think we have spread glitter and gold dust everywhere, but the truth is when you see with elfin eyes you realize it is the very Earth that shines.

The Call of Faerie makes one feel like one is falling in Love, which one is.

There are magic rings, magic swords, magic keys and many other objects of magic, but there is nothing that is quite as powerful and magical as love.

Faerie houses are like little shrines that call the spirit of Faerie, bringing it into the world.

Every elf descends from the royal line of Faerie and ascends toward the Divine Magic.

"It is not the shadows that create the light but the light that creates the shadows." Olde Elven Saying meaning: Intelligent and enlightened folk are more apt to be eccentric and vice versa.

We elves may hide sometimes, but only because it is wise to do so, we are proud to be elfin.

Some folks think we elves hate dwarves. That is not true. We don't hate them, although we have been known to look down on them.

An elf can express more with a smile than most folks can say with a thousand words.

Elves are like the morning mists standing before the rising sun whispering there is mystery in life still and ever will be.

You don't have to prove you're an elf to anyone. You just need to be your own 'elf.

Elfland does not create elves, elves create Elfland.

The Fountain of Youth springs from the heart of Faerie.

"YOU MUST MOST OFTEN SEEK FAERIE TO FIND FAERIE BUT YOU WILL ALMOST NEVER FIND FAERIE BY SEEKING IT, RATHER IT WILL FIND YOU.".

. . . .

If you wish to understand the elves, gaze at the mist and let your imagination wander to places of wonder.

Hurry not to find Faerie but gentle be your way for Faerie functions on its own time and will find you when it is ready.

Faerie created the elves so the elves could create Elfin.

Elves don't judge books by their covers nor covers by the book.

If you eliminate everything from your life that others don't approve of, you will wind up being nothing.

If the cities belong to man, then the forest wild surely belongs to the Faerie Folk.

When one is an elf, one is an elf from the crown of one's head to the tip of one's toes.

Life is relationship.

When elves come together, both the world and they are transformed.

While not all of Faerie is safe, there are safe refuges in Faerie.

We are always ours'elves yet ever becoming. This is a mystery of the Universe and our elven nature.

The truth of our souls is written on our bodies.

Elves love stories. Particularly stories about elves and magic. That may seem egocentric but we don't care. We like what we like.

When we elves say we are going to do things "by the book", we're usually speaking of a fantasy novel.

"It's not the clothes that make an elf, but the elf that makes the clothes."
—Old Elven Saying

What Elves Say About Costumes and Dress

"IT IS SAID THAT MOST WOMAN LOVE A MAN IN UNIFORM. ELVES LOVE AN ELF IN COSTUME." . . . . .

The Spirit does not have a dress code.
—Old Elven Saying

Fashion among the elven seems to be divided between two main styles: 1) those who dress very plainly in simple outfits of cotton, hemp, linen and wool; and 2) those who are forever decked out in velvet, lace, silk and brocade.

Even when we elfin live in poverty, we tend to have access to abundance. This is most of all because we have each other. For instance, while we are quite poor, in the view of the world, we could, if we choose, never wear the same clothes twice, simply tossing each set or giving them away after we've worn them. For clothes easily come to us for free in a never ending supply. Of course, we don't only wear clothes once. Not because it would be frivolous to do so, but because we have our favorites of velvet, silk and rayon and we tend to wear them until they are tattered rags, we love them so.

Elves have little concept of high fashion or low fashion,
Nor do they care about what is popular.
Their interest is always on unique style.

We elves are not required to wear traditional elven raiment. Running around naked is also perfectly acceptable.

Modern elves often view our attire as an advertisement saying: Welcome All Elf Folk!"

Elves consider dress to be an aspect of free speech and our right to costume as we please should be protected.

Facts About Elves

"We elves don't exactly have saints, but if we did Tolkien would certainly be one of them.". . . . .

When asked who we elves worship, we reply, "We worship each other."

We elves are created by our own magic.

Our love is ever given freely. It is our enmity that will cost you.

The many tales that say that we elves kidnap mortals and keep them imprisoned in Faerie against their will are utterly false. One can not stay in Faerie unless their whole heart desires it.

People sometimes meet us and are disappointed. We are not what they imagined us to be. But then, they were not really looking for us, but for their own true s'elves and until they find thems'elves they will never find us.

It was not easy deciding to be born and raised among men, but it seemed the only way to help them transform from savages to gentlemen.

Elves show respect to all beings, both those who have earned it and those who can profit from our example.

We are not looking to find elven in the future, but to create it now.

People sometimes try to jerk our chain and then they discover we don't have one.

Some people ever wish to limit us. They say we can't be elves or faeries because of this, that, or the other thing. However, it is in the nature of elves to ignore such rantings.

If you wish to find elves, look for those who love all things magical, elven and of faerie kind.

"WHAT MOST CALL PRAYER, WE CALL EVOCATION.".....

<u>A Very Special Fact About Elves:</u> Many people believe that harmony is achieved through conflict. That two dualities battle it out until a merger is at last reached. We elves believe in harmony through diversity. The mutual acceptance and appreciation of differences in styles, beliefs and taste.

Elves equate cruelty with ignorance, although they can be very firm when dealing with miscreants, but are ever courteous when doing so. The point in their minds is not one of establishing superiority or dominance but of creating balance and just order.

Elves seek to create a new and better world by living our lives as though it already existed.

Realities of Elfin: "Some Christians may not approve of us, but there is no doubt in our minds that Jesus does."

Elves are not the sort to take orders without question, which is why they make bad soldiers but great warriors.

Elves are catalytic by nature. We adapt to every situation and then slowly transform it to everyone's greater advantage.

Elves are at one and the same time the most individual and community orient folk, for the community endeavors to empower every individual and every individual seeks to empower all their others

Living with elves is like living with old, wise children.

It is the goal of nearly all elven to make life more wondrous and magical for everyone.

The reason we elven don't express our opinions as though they were absolute truth is because we've changed our minds so many times when we've encountered greater evidence and reasoning that adaptability and open mindedness have become an integral part of our character.

"Everyone is limited by one's own nature." —Olde Elven Saying.

"Even the rocks stand in their way."
—An Old Elven Saying, meaning the All of Nature opposes it.

Whispers of an Elven Enchantress

"FOR THE ELVES, ENCHANTMENT IS LIKE THE BREATH OF FAERIE DANCING THROUGH OUR SOULS." . . . .

The elves say Enchantment can speak volumes without ever uttering a word.

Imagination is in many ways the source, the goal and the result of enchantment.

Enchantment is both a means to an end and the end.

The more one practices enchantment, the easier and the more enjoyable it becomes.

The elves say that if you wish to understand enchantment, then listen to a baby's laughter or make a baby smile.

Enchantment is a magic that is soft as a whisper and more powerful than thunder.

Enchantment is like the wind from the ocean bending trees as they grow.

If we repeat ourselves, it's a chant; if we rhyme, it is a spell; and if we add a bit of music, it's a magic we know well. If we do all three together, it's enchantment at it's core that dances through the Faerie night now and evermore.

Enchantment is a power that not only bears the responsibility of using it wisely, but also to enjoy its use.

If you wish to find Faerie, follow the trail of enchantment, the stronger it is the closer you are. If you wish to step into Faerie, practice enchantment; the more enchanting you are the quicker it will come to find you.

With magic, you can gain power, wealth and fame. With enchantment, you can gain everything.

"While we admire courage and bravery, for elves the greatest heroes are the artists, poets, writers, and musicians." —What Elves Say

More of What the Elves Say

"IT IS UNWISE TO CATEGORIZE ELVES TOO MUCH, FOR WE ARE MYRIAD AND VARIED BEYOND IMAGINING.". . . . .

We elves don't worships gods, we commune with Nature which is Divine and Magical.

We are born elfin, but in this world it is sometimes years before we awaken and put a name to what we've always felt about ours'elves.

Normal folk wear uniforms; elfin folk wear costumes.

In Elfin, every house is beautiful.

Elves always pick up pennies when we find them. To us, all found things are magic.

The Elven say: "If you are going to be serious, make sure it is something worth being serious about."

To those who are not of our kind, our realms can look mysterious, dangerous and uninviting. But to we elfin, it is as cozy as can be.

Some people think we are wee folk. Others think we elves are quite tall. Some believe we live in this world. Still others believe we abide in another dimension. All these things are true. We are all of this and much, much more.

The fact that elves, wizards and witches are often portrayed as wearing pointy hats and shoes points to the reality that we live with a purpose and that purpose is to re-enchant the world.

The pathways through Faerie are ever changing. You must set your heart on where you truly wish to go and then they will take you there.

The Elven say: "Be vulnerable to those who are open and honest, be prepared for those who are not."

"YOU WILL FIND US IN THE FORESTS, EVEN WHEN YOU DON'T SEE US THERE. FOR THE FORESTS ARE FILLED WITH MYSTERY AND WHEREVER ENCHANTMENT ABIDES SO DOES FAERIE." . . . . .

Some folks like to tickle people's ribs. Some like to tickle their feet. Elves like to tickle people's fancy.

The Elves say: "Have Faith; and Reason."
The Elves say: "Have Faith and Reason."
The Elves say: "Have Faith in Reason."

Among some elves the weavers of the Fates are viewed as an Ancient Witch known as the Necromancer who carries a crystal ball, removes disused cobwebs with her broom and rules the Past. The Present is dominated by a bald middle aged male who carries a staff and does martial arts katas while reciting spells. He is known as the Dancer. And the Future is created by an androgynous child who plays with figures in a sand box imagining the future into being. No one knows this one's name, although some call Hir Starlight.

The deep secrets of elfin magic cannot be found in books, however, books do hold the keys to the imagination where the most profound secrets dwell.

Elves toast with toast, which we dip in tea or wine, rather like the Communion. It makes perfect sense to us. Why else would it be called a toast?

If we were as great as we were meant to be, we'd have saved the Earth and set all kind free, but we haven't given up trying.

Vampires become immortal through the sharing of blood. Elves become immortal through the sharing of the sacred waters of Elfin, the Fountain of Youth that we call the Kiss of the Immortals.

The Elves Say: "To the elven, trees are family."

Our bodies may age but our elven spirits are ever young. This is not just something we say but the reality of our true elfin nature.

"WHEN WE ELVES SAY WE AWAIT YOU IN FAERIE, WE MEAN RIGHT HERE, RIGHT NOW." . . . . .

When you find Faerie within you, you discover it all around you.

A warm fire, a cozy gathering with good friends, and a sky filled with stars are all ingredients of Elven Magic.

The Mystery is One and Two and Many and All at the same time, which is Eternally Now.

Normal folk see the world of illusion or appearance. Elves see that world and the energetic and radiant world that lives within and behind it.

Enchantment is as natural to elves as swimming is to mermaids.

Some people believe that true love is a fairy tale. It is, indeed. It is one of the greatest faerie magics ever created and we elves strive to manifest it every day.

Elves are different. We're different from normal folk. We're different from each other. We're each unique and eccentric. That's what makes us all the same.

Elves shower blessings upon our friends and ever wish to be friends with everyone and so those who insist on being our enemies are viewed as being especially ignorant.

For Elves, Halloween is a time to be ours'elves. Just like always.

One doesn't have to be crazy to see Faerie, although those still in the normal world will think you so. In truth, it is those who are quite sane who live in Faerie and see the world more truly than most can bear.

The Elven say: "Sour Grapes do not make for a good Whine."

Special Elf Quotes

ॐ

"If we elves say the same thing twice,
it is because it was worth repeating,
although we will nearly always try to say
it in a new and innovative way.
If we say it exactly the same, it is a chant.
If it rhymes, it is a spell.
If we sing, it is an enchantment.
If you start to sway,
it is a magic most amazing."
—The Silver Elves

"It is hard to say how long we might stay among you,
for the choice is not entirely our own.
We ours'elves are neither great nor important
but we have come bearing gifts from the Spirits
of the Stars and from the very heart of Elfin.
We bring a feather shed from the wing
of the dove of peace,
and seeds descended from the sacred trees of Elfin,
and a spark from the Eternal Silver Flame,
which gave birth to all the Eldar folk.
And while some will not accept it and others see it not,
and others still will attempt to blow it out,
it is a Flame Eternal and even extinguished it will
awaken again from its very ashes and find a place in
every heart that longs still for the beauty
and magic of Faerie."
—The Silver Elves

*"Many people write that we elfin
envy man his mortal life,
because man, realizing he's going to die,
somehow experiences life fully and savors it the more.
This is the most incredible nonsense.
Not only because we experience life
just as deeply and passionately,
although perhaps not as emotionally, as man;
but, also because we in no way envy man's mortality.
Nor, in fact, do we pity him.
We are simply waiting for them to realize
what we've been telling them all along,
that they are immortal, too."*
—The Silver Elves

"Elves are not much inclined toward creating cities,
But if we did so
They would be largely indistinguishable from the forests
That surrounded them.
The Buildings would tend to be unique
But all nearly obscured by leaves and ivy and vines
And they would be lined with fruit and nut trees
That all may share,
Especially the itinerant among us."
—The Silver Elves

About the Authors

The Silver Elves The Silver Elves, Zardoa and Silver Flame, are a family of elves who have been living and sharing the Elven Way since 1975. They are the authors of 36 books on magic and enchantment, including:

The Book of Elven Runes: A Passage Into Faerie;

The Magical Elven Love Letters, volume I, 2, and 3;

An Elfin Book of Spirits: Evoking the Beneficent Powers of Faerie;

Caressed by an Elfin Breeze: The Poems of Zardoa Silverstar;

Eldafaryn: True Tales of Magic from the Lives of the Silver Elves;

Arvyndase (Silverspeech): A Short Course in the Magical Language of the Silver Elves;

The Elven Book of Dreams: A Magical Oracle of Faerie;

The Book of Elven Magick: The Philosophy and Enchantments of the Seelie Elves, Volume 1 & 2;

What An Elf Would Do: A Magical Guide to the Manners and Etiquette of the Faerie Folk;

The Elven Tree of Life Eternal: A Magical Quest for One's True S'Elf;

Magic Talks: On Being a Correspondence Between the Silver Elves and the Elf Queen's Daughters;

Sorcerers' Dialogues: A Further Correspondence Between the Silver Elves and the Founders of the Elf Queen's Daughters;

Discourses on High Sorcery: More Correspondence Between the Silver Elves and the Founders of the Elf Queen's Daughters;

Ruminations on Necromancy: Continuing Correspondence Between the Silver Elves and the Founders of the Elf Queen's Daughter;

The Elven Way: The Magical Path of the Shining Ones;

The Book of Elf Names: 5,600 Elven Names to Use for Magic, Game Playing, Inspiration, Naming One's Self and One's Child, and as Words in the Elven Language of the Silver Elves;

Elven Silver: The Irreverent Faery Tales of Zardoa Silverstar;

An Elven Book of Ryhmes: Book Two of the Magical Poems of Zardoa Silverstar;

The Voice of Faerie: Making Any Tarot Deck Into an Elven Oracle;

Liber Aelph: Words of Guidance from the Silver Elves to our Magical Children;

The Shining Ones: The Elfin Spirits That Guide You According to Your Birth Date and the Evolutionary Lessons They Offer;

Living the Personal Myth: Making the Magic of Faerie Real in One's Own Personal Life;

Elf Magic Mail, The Original Letters of the Elf Queen's Daughters with Comentary by the Silver Elves, Book 1 and 2;

The Elves of Lyndarys: A Magical Tale of Modern Faerie Folk;

The Elf Folk's Book of Cookery: Recipes For a Delighted Tongue, a Healthy Body and a Magical Life;

Faerie Unfolding: The Cosmic Expression of the Divine Magic;

The Elements of Elven Magic: A New View of Calling the Elementals Based Upon the Periodic Table of Elements and

The Keys to Elfin Enchantment: Mastery of the Faerie Light Through the Portals of Manifestation.

The Silver Elves have had various articles published in *Circle Network News Magazine* and have given out over 6,000 elven names to interested individuals in the Arvyndase language, with each elf name having a unique meaning specifically for that person. They are also mentioned numerous times in *Not In Kansas Anymore* by Christine Wicker (Harper San Francisco, 2005), and *A Field Guide to Otherkin* by Lupa (Megalithica Books, 2007). An interview with the Silver Elves is also included in Emily Carding's recent book *Faery Craft.*

The Silver Elves understand the world as a magical or miraculous phenomena, and that all beings, by pursuing their own true path, will become whomever they truly desire to be. You are welcome to visit their website at http://silverelves@live.com and to join them on Facebook with names "Michael J. Love (Zardoa of The SilverElves)" and "Martha Char Love (SilverFlame of The SilverElves)."

www.ingramcontent.com/pod-product-compliance
Lightning Source LLC
Chambersburg PA
CBHW081830280526
45789CB00007B/2410